Miller Center Series on the American Presidency

America's Unwritten Constitution

AMERICA'S UNWRITTEN CONSTITUTION

Science, Religion, and Political Responsibility

DON K. PRICE

Louisiana State University Press / Baton Rouge and London

Designer: Albert Crochet
Typeface: Linotron Trump Mediaeval
Typesetter: Graphic Composition, Inc.
Printer: Thomson-Shore, Inc.
Binder: John H. Dekker & Sons, Inc.

LIBRARY OF CONGRESS CATALOGING IN PUBLICATION DATA

Price, Don Krasher.
    America's unwritten constitution.

    (Miller Center series on the American Presidency)
    Bibliography: p.
    Includes index.
    1. Separation of powers—United States—History.
    2. United States—Constitutional history.   3. Church
    and state—United States—History.   4. Science and
        state—United States—History.   I. Title.   II. Series.
JK305.P87   1983   320.473   83-5439
                ISBN 0-8071-1119-8

For Hattie

Contents

Foreword

With this book, the Miller Center of Public Affairs at the University of Virginia continues a sponsored series of analytic works on the American presidency.

These works represent the scholarship of those whose research and writing have been encouraged by the center and who have participated as visiting scholars in the center's Program on the Presidency. Through this program, the center undertakes to contribute to the building of a new science of the presidency for our time. The focus is on the study of the organs and philosophies of central power and leadership in the American constitutional system; the underlying concern is how to reconcile the need for effective central leadership with the constitutional imperatives of limited government and divided but shared power—particularly under twentieth-century conditions. Three main areas of inquiry are embraced in the center's presidency program. One is concerned with the nature and purposes of the presidency as an instrumentality of governance and of leadership in its larger institutional, political, cultural, and historical setting. A second area of inquiry concentrates on particular problems in which the presidency is deeply involved or which carry far-reaching implications for the conduct and organization of the office. A third area of inquiry concentrates on the study of individual presidencies to learn what lessons may be drawn from the past.

Drawing on a lifetime of experience and study, Don K. Price examines the problems of leadership and governance in the United States and Great Britain against the background of their differing "political, cultural and historical settings." An active participant in certain landmark reforms including those initiated by the President's Committee on Administrative Management in 1937 and by the Commission on the Organization of the Executive Branch of 1948, Price reviews their assumptions and consequences, and those of later efforts, in the light of recent history. As a past president of the American Association for the Advancement of Science, he assesses contributions and limitations of science and public administration in the strengthening of the nation's capacity to govern itself. He does not shrink from inquiring into such troublesome issues as the sources of authority for governing in the United States, certain underlying philosophies of human nature and politics, dissent in American religion and politics, accountability under the unwritten constitution and the relationship between the institutional presidency and the cabinet. The result is a treatise of enduring value as rich in insights on political philosophy as on the principles of American government.

Don K. Price was a visiting scholar at the Miller Center in the spring of 1981. During this period, he sketched in the main outline and commenced the writing of *America's Unwritten Constitution: Science, Religion, and Political Responsibility.*

KENNETH W. THOMPSON, Director,
Miller Center of Public Affairs

JAMES STERLING YOUNG, Director of
the Program on the Presidency

Preface

When President Carter's Commission for a National Agenda acknowledged in 1980 that it had none of the optimism shown by President Eisenhower's Commission on Goals for Americans in 1960, it summed up a basic change in the political mood of Americans.

The earlier confidence, following the defeat of the Nazis and Fascists, had evaporated. We were no longer so sure that if we revised our political system in democratic directions our government could take care of the threats of nuclear war, environmental pollution, the loss of energy, or genetic and psychological manipulation. We had come to distrust not only our earlier prescriptions for political reform and our confidence in presidential leadership, but also our faith in a rational and scientific method for dealing with public issues. More people began to vote for reactionary political formulas and to lose confidence in the ability of government to manage the economy. And many thoughtful observers (and some practitioners) of politics began to question the adequacy of an eighteenth-century Constitution to deal with contemporary problems.

When twenty years ago I gave a series of lectures at the University of Virginia that were revised and published as *The Scientific Estate*, I was concerned mainly with the need to understand the ways in which the sciences were related to the political system. But the events since then have made it clear that, for all of the importance of the sciences to our present difficulties, a much broader approach needs to be taken, and in greater historical depth, if we are to learn how to deal with our major problems. For the key concern now is not how science and technology can make more efficient the administration of our policies but how conflicts arising out of competing scientific specialties may be resolved under some system of constitutional accountability.

It was too easy an assumption on the part of the liberals that if science could determine the one best way the only obstacle would be selfish business interests. That faith was as futile as the opposite belief that the free play of the market was adequate to protect the public. If anyone undertakes to devise a system for the better coordination of public policy, he will find it opposed, not merely by selfish private interests, but even more effectively from within the government by bureaucratic specialists and congressional committees. To understand how such political complications developed, it seems to me that we need to explore the attitudes toward established authority that were first developed by religious dissenters, given institutional form by the lawyers, and then taken over by modern scientists and their professional allies.

I was very happy when again the University of Virginia gave me an opportunity to reflect on this range of problems by an appointment as a visiting scholar at the Miller Center of Public Affairs in the spring of 1981. The aura of Thomas Jefferson's concern for the contribution of science to free institutions makes Charlottesville the ideal setting for renewed reflection on a perennial subject. I had contributed a paper, "The Institutional Presidency and the Unwritten Constitution," to a conference that had been held there in 1980, and part of that paper has been revised for inclusion in this book. To various faculty members of the Miller Center and especially to its director, Kenneth W. Thompson, and the director of its Presidency Program, James S. Young, I am grateful for many helpful criticisms and suggestions as well as for their hospitality and encouragement.

Since my topic deals with such a broad range of subjects and with comparisons with other constitutional systems, I have depended heavily on the advice and criticism of many friends.

On the comparisons with Great Britain and Canada, I benefited greatly from the advice of Lord Trend, who since his retirement as cabinet secretary in the United Kingdom has been rector of Lincoln College, Oxford; of Sir Edgar Williams, formerly warden of Rhodes House and editor of the *Dictionary of National Biography*; and of Michael Pitfield, secretary of the Cabinet and clerk of the Privy Council of Canada.

In dealing with the interaction of the natural sciences with government, I continued to draw heavily on the help of my colleagues Harvey Brooks, I. Bernard Cohen, and Gerald Holton, all of whom have been led far beyond their original specialized disciplines in the hardest sciences by their concerns with the history, philosophy, and ethical dilemmas of modern science.

I am especially indebted to Alan Heimert for his criticism and counsel on the religious contribution to American political thought during the colonial period, and to James Luther Adams, Howard L. Brooks, and Thomas J. Stritch for general advice on the relation of theological ideas to governmental affairs.

My colleagues at Harvard University and in the National Academy of Public Administration whose help on problems of government was invaluable are too numerous to list. But I should mention especially Samuel H. Beer, Dan H. Fenn, Jr., Hugh Heclo, and Richard E. Neustadt, all of whom read and criticized the entire manuscript, and others who counseled me on various specific chapters, among them Avis DeVoto, Frederick C. Mosher, Adam Ulam, and James E. Webb.

As I tried to make use of all this help from various authorities on so wide a range of subject matter, I had invaluable aid and comfort during the entire job of writing and revision from Shirley F. Brooks, who had helped me with the research and composition of my last book and had the patience and fortitude to join with me again on this one. Her skill and thoroughness are the best guarantee that any remaining errors in the manuscript are my own.

My colleague Hugh Heclo, as he read an early draft of this book, challenged me on one specific point: "Why," he said, "don't you admit that you were involved in that issue? You didn't make up your mind about it by reading the article you cite in that footnote." As I thought about his comment, I decided that he was right, and about many more parts of the manuscript than he realized. While I have tried to be objective in my analysis and to give references in the following notes that will help the reader check up on my opinions, I may as well admit my personal involvement—most often as a student or at a very junior staff level in government—in many of the problems that I am discussing. Accordingly, the notes to each chapter are preceded by an account of the events that led me to take a continuing interest in these problems and that may account for the biases in my opinions about them.

America's Unwritten Constitution

Introduction

The Confused Sources of Authority

As we approach in the United States the third century of our Constitution, we are becoming less confident that our system of government is adequate to deal with the difficult problems ahead. Science, once considered the guarantor of perpetual progress, now seems (along with the technology it has developed) more like a threat to civilization through the possibilities of genetic and psychological manipulation, the pollution of the environment, and the potential for nuclear conflict. And religion, which was presumed to be no political problem as long as church and state were safely separated, seems to be becoming a more disturbing force in politics.

Rather more dangerous than the specific problems themselves is our loss of any consensus—even within any one of the major contending intellectual or political factions—on how to approach the problems. We are confused about what government should do, how it should do it, and how we may hold it responsible for what it does.

The so-called liberals, who from the days of the New Deal to the Great Society had supported the extension of programs of social service, were inclined to build their case on the ideas of the social scientists. While it was absurd for members of Congress to accuse philanthropic foundations of Communist sympathies for their support of the social sciences, that support surely contributed to the intellectual climate in which a welfare state could flourish.[1] But now the liberals have become skeptical about the ability of government to carry out the programs which they legislated into existence and dismayed by the unintended and perverse consequences of some of those that seemed most successful.

The so-called conservatives, eager for a renewed commitment to free enterprise, are still forced to accept the need for government action to stimulate or direct the economy. As they do so, they abandon the old conservative view that government should be managed like the traditional business corporation, with a neat hierarchical organization and all its costs shown in a single budget. With some uneasiness they undertake to control the economy by indirect means, using monetary incentives and tax exemptions rather than appropriated funds and contracts with private corporations rather than full-time civil servants to effect public policy. And the old tools of planning and propaganda that for so long served the cause of scientific and progressive political reformers—the academic research institutions, the "think tanks," and the political action groups—are now multiplied and more richly endowed by the backers of conservative programs.

The academic supporters of political reform are now inclined to regret their measures that have weakened discipline within the parties and increased the tendency of members of Congress to think for themselves and vote as their several constituencies please. At the same time, for all their reverence for the memory of FDR and what he did to strengthen the chief executive, they are coming to regret that the President, as a national leader, has been saddled with the detailed burdens of the management of the executive departments.

Conservative politicians, on the other hand, now seem prepared to accept a strong presidency as the only way to produce weak government. Presidential leadership, under President Reagan at least as much as President Carter, means the public assertion of a kind of personal influence by staff members of the Executive Office that would have shocked Speaker Rayburn or Senator Taft.

A free citizenry can hold government responsible only if it can choose from time to time which elected officers should hold power and what the limits of that power should be. It can do so only if the contending political leaders, while disagreeing on policies, agree in large measure to maintain government as a going concern and to respect the legal processes by which they hold or give up their power. This general conception was responsible for maintaining the rule of law, and for protecting the subordinate administrative staff from too much political corruption. The separation of policy from administration, with the legislators controlling policy and the executive agencies being managed as much like private business as possible, was for years taken as the ideal.

This economy-and-efficiency approach, on which reformers have relied for many years, provided the zeal that supported the work of the two Commissions on the Organization of the Executive Branch, chaired by former president Hoover in 1948 and 1954, whose members in part of their work were fortunately able to rise above the principles of their backers and take a broader view. It was an approach that had made much sense as long as the programs of government were separate and distinct efforts to supplement the private economy—welfare benefits or regulatory activities that were visualized as independent entities to be managed with as little "overlapping and duplication" as possible. But in a technological and industrial society, everything is related to everything else. Energy problems are problems of the environment, which in turn is one of public health. Transportation problems are those of industrial productivity and the structure of cities, which in turn are problems of employment, welfare payments, and of course, fiscal and monetary policy. The internal efficiency of each of the separate programs is less of a problem than the conflicts or cooperation among them.

President Carter's Commission for a National Agenda for the Eighties diagnosed the principal political difficulty of the United States as one of a general fragmentation of institutions, in political parties, the Congress, and the executive alike. In particular, it singled out the civil service as being notably deficient in a sense of general responsibility or a broad perspective. President Reagan's administration, while understandably giving no credit to his predecessor's commission, from the outset made a far stronger effort to patch together the kind of political and managerial discipline that might create a more coherent policy.

At this point, we need to ask not only what government should do, how government should do it, and how we can hold government responsible for what it does but also a more difficult and fundamental question: how can we know what we should do and how we should do it and how we may hold government responsible? That is to say, what is the authoritative source of truth on which we should rely?

In a scholarly sense, the answer to that question had seemed obvious for several generations: science was the reliable source of knowledge and the engine of progress, even if it had to be supplemented by value judgments during our stage of imperfect comprehension. From the days of Thomas Jefferson and John Adams and Benjamin Franklin to President Hoover's Committee on Social Trends and Vannevar Bush's *Science, the Endless Frontier*, even the lay public with little comprehension of scientific method was not disposed to quarrel with the assumption that science was leading us in the right direction. But during the past generation there has been a sharp break with this tradition; the old faith in science as a system by which the accumulation of new facts would lead to new knowledge and support endless social progress has been shaken by the misapplied notions of relativity and indeterminacy—abstractions which confuse the public and shake its faith in social consensus and political freedom.[2] Accordingly the alliance between liberal or radical or progressive intellectuals and the community of science has been badly split, if not destroyed. And religious groups, which intellectuals had written off as political forces ever since the repeal of Prohibition, have begun to exert influence in unanticipated and confusing ways, with populist evangelical sects supporting causes commonly considered reactionary and the Jesuit order being disciplined by the Pope for radicalism.

At a more practical level, the old studies of public administration have begun to be supplanted by an approach with greater scientific depth—the new intellectual tools of policy analysis, which had been developed since the Second World War by the economists and other social scientists, originally for the study of military problems. With these techniques, we have begun to understand some of the complex issues involving the interaction of government programs, the "trade-offs" among them. This approach has helped to identify many troubles that support the growing skepticism about the efficacy of governmental actions, especially in regulatory programs. When various zealous specialists undertook to solve separate social problems by separate actions, good analysis often showed that the total effect might be counterproductive: minimum wage laws might restrict youth employment or rigid safety codes might add unreasonably to the cost of housing or strict bans on carcinogens might deprive diabetic or obese patients of a comparatively safe sweetener like saccharin. On the other hand, policy analysis has sometimes pointed the way to a more satisfactory synthesis of related programs, so as to accomplish—insofar as science can measure utilitarian benefits—the greatest good for the greatest number. Such calculations, however, might well be ineffective for either of two reasons.

The first has to do with our previous question—the system of enforcing responsibility or accountability. We may often find that there is no center of political authority in existence with the capacity to put into effect a rational comprehensive policy. The United States government is not a single rational actor. The degree of independence of congressional committees and their staffs and the related independence of specialized executive bureaus and agencies make it impossible to plan and carry out a coherent program. There is no clear center of authority in either the Congress or the executive that the voters can hold responsible.

If we are confident that our analytic and scientific techniques give complete answers to policy questions, we may then well assume that the constitutional system—including legislative processes and administrative institutions—should be adjusted so as to produce greater unity and discipline in the present incoherent system.

But our intellectual leaders have lost much of their confidence in the adequacy of the scientific and analytic approach, and this is the second reason for their skepticism about granting full authority to a single political power. We are faced not only with the skepticism of the lay public, motivated in part by religious revivalism to distrust science, but also with the critiques of moral philosophers, who argue that the techniques of policy analysis, while indispensable as the first step toward understanding a major policy issue, are unable to deal with several of its major aspects. Utilitarian calculations of the greatest good for the greatest number cannot deal with such questions as the rights of minorities, which must not be overridden in the average interests of the majority. What rights, regardless of cost, are inalienable? What standards of distributive justice demand that those at the bottom of the economic heap must be given benefits even if to do so reduces the average welfare of the population as a whole? And most important, when must utilitarian calculations be disregarded in order to protect freedom and to avoid too great a concentration of political power within the nation?

Such questions as these set up an apparent conflict between our desire to make government more responsible, which may justify granting its political head a wider range of legal authority and administrative discretion, and our desire to protect the freedom of individuals and the interests of regional, ethnic, or economic minorities. As American government, in order to deal with problems of the economy and of national security, has broadened its role in national life, it has had to tighten up its system of responsibility, usually by delegating greater authority to the President—for example, in his authority over the organization of departments and agencies, over their personnel systems, and over their budgets. The model we have often imitated has been the British government, which has not been encumbered by our system of separate elections and independent tenure of the members of Congress and the President. We note with admiration that the Parliament has the legal power to hold the Prime Minister and Cabinet accountable at any moment by a vote of no confidence, and the executive leadership in the meantime has authority over both the policies and administration of the government to a degree that astounds American politicians.

Accordingly, as political reformers look for ways to make American government more accountable, once they are persuaded that the business corporation is no longer an appropriate model, they are tempted to return to the classic ideal that has intrigued them for more than a century: the parliamentary system of the United Kingdom. In that government the disciplined parties, the unification of powers, and the Cabinet and its network of committees, have been subjects of fascinated study by those who want more discipline and integrity in American public policy. This comparison has been a recurrent obsession in American political arguments ever since John

Adams and Alexander Hamilton argued whether the British constitution was successful in spite of its corruptions or because of them. The young Woodrow Wilson's *Congressional Government* proposed something like an imitation of the British parliamentary system, and more recently such authorities as Thomas K. Finletter, William Y. Elliott, E. S. Corwin, Henry Reuss, and Lloyd Cutler have followed suit.[3]

It would not do to dismiss this line of thinking because Great Britain is no longer the dominant power it was in the Victorian era or because recent social and economic changes have greatly weakened the unity of each of the major parties on which effective parliamentary responsibility depended. Neither conservative nor socialist governments have been able during the past decade or two to maintain a steady and coherent policy against the divisive influences of the scramble for subsidies by business and for pay raises by competing factions of labor. But in view of the grave difficulties that these conflicts have caused in the political system, it is all the more remarkable how much the institutional habits and administrative structure of Her Majesty's Government have held the system together with more coherence than America's diffuse structure can demonstrate.[4] Moreover the parliamentary and administrative institutions of the United Kingdom have set an admirable example for free governments everywhere, perhaps especially because they have been supported by a truly conservative tradition—the line of thought from Burke to Churchill which saw politics and public service as the primary moral obligation of the nation's elite and a strong government as the safeguard of traditional liberties.

But it is pertinent to ask whether the quality of British parliamentary institutions comes from its central structural feature, the unification of powers, which another country could imitate (as many have done) by Constitutional amendment, or from traditional attitudes and institutional habits that are more difficult to adopt by legal action. If we think about the recent experience of Italy, where the parliamentary system upsets, on the average, more than one government each year, to say nothing of Iran, where the real power that displaced the Shah was neither the President nor the Prime Minister, it is easy to see that the formal structure of parliament and prime minister is not enough to produce a free and responsible system. Even France and Germany, in order to develop relatively stable parliamentary systems, had to abolish the central feature of the British system (the complete subordination of all policy to the Parliament through the Cabinet) and either to grant real power to a separately chosen chief of state or to limit the freedom of the parliament to dismiss the prime minister.

Obviously a great deal depends not on formal legal structure but on political habits and the social context. Even so, we may still learn a great deal by comparing the workings of the American system with those of countries that are more or less similar in tradition and social environment. Hence it may be useful to consider not only the British system but also the experience of Canada, which is less like the United Kingdom and more like the United States in its continental size and federal structure.

It is also suggestive that the more aggressively egalitarian political factions in the U.K. are now advocating imitation of the U.S. legislative procedures and administrative methods as zealously as any Americans ever advocated imitating those of the British. It is not very likely that either nation will make a fundamental constitutional change in imitation of the other. An amendment to the American Constitution that would abolish the President as the chief executive is about as likely, one might suppose, as an amendment to end the income tax and much less likely than one to outlaw abortion. But in two ways the U.S. may benefit from a study of the British system.

First, such a study can provide a clearer idea of the ways in which individual and minority rights are either threatened or protected by executive authority or by the concentration of political leadership in the legislature. Correspondingly, we can discover how much their protection depends on Constitutional checks and balances. Civil rights in the United Kingdom have been protected and the interests of minorities taken into account by processes different from those in the United States.

Second, it may be possible to learn why it is that, when the United States undertakes to imitate a British precedent, the experiment goes wrong. The United States established its civil service and budgetary systems and its institutional procedures for coordinating national security programs—the National Security Council—in direct imitation of British institutions. Unfortunately, none of them worked out to look like their models. Nothing in the U.S. Constitution required such a disappointing outcome.

The roots of the incoherence of policy which lead many critics to wish to amend the U.S. Constitution do not come from the Constitution but rather from the unwritten constitution—the fixed political customs that have developed without formal Constitutional amendment, but that have been authorized by statute or frozen, at least temporarily, in tradition. The party conventions and the primary system, congressional committees and their staffs, the statutory structure of executive departments, the Executive Office of the President, the press conference and television coverage, and freedom of information—none of these was established by the Constitution or foreseen by its framers, and all could be abolished without formal amendment. It would be impossible for a parliamentary cabinet system to work properly without some change in all these aspects of the U.S. unwritten constitution, and if they could be altered informally a parliamentary system might not be needed, even to accomplish a drastic coordination of policy. How drastic the U.S. should want such coordination to be is another question that we may consider later.

The unwritten constitution, even more than the written one, is a reflection of the basic political philosophy of the people, a reflection of their traditional prejudices and attitudes, often incoherent and not explicitly formulated by the average citizen or, in the U.K., by the average subject of the Queen—and a gulf of prejudice and tradition lies between those who think of themselves as citizens and those, as subjects. That gulf has been narrowing in some ways in recent years. But to understand the difference between the unwritten constitutions of the two countries requires one to back up and consider the ways in which their political thought separated into quite different streams about the time of the American Revolution. The main issue had to do with what the public considers the proper source of basic authority and, behind that authority, the ultimate source of truth for the resolution of great public issues. It is this kind of belief and not a mechanical process of votes of confidence or dissolution of a legislature that makes the fundamental difference.

When the English held out in the era of the Enlightenment against adopting a republican constitution, it was not because the idea had never occurred to them. On the contrary, it was because they had tried one and disliked it intensely. The first political revolution of modern times—the seventeenth-century Puritan revolution that beheaded King Charles and did so much to stimulate the settlement of the American colonies—put England (and Scotland and Ireland as well) for a time under a written constitution with a republican ruler and subject to the domination of a strict religious dogma or, at any rate, a series of competing popular dogmas.

From the Restoration of King Charles II in 1660 to the Reform Bills of the nineteenth century, the British parliamentary system evolved as a reaction against the Puritan Commonwealth experience. As it did so, it developed two prejudices—we may almost call them constitutional principles: first, it is safer to accept the judgment of a ruling establishment with respect to the organization and procedures of government than to let elected legislators make detailed decisions; and second, in any policy decision the judgment of politicians or administrative generalists is a safer guide than religious zeal or the precise but narrow truths of experts.

American politics, as it evolved after 1776, had a different style. The American Revolution had been supported by zealous religious dissenters who wanted to abolish all establishments and substitute a rule of law. Political issues have been discussed ever since in moralistic and legalistic terms that more pragmatic countries find confusing. The leaders of the Revolution included those with a strong commitment to the advancement of science, in the best Enlightenment tradition; ever since, it has been tempting to look to science for answers to policy questions and easier to support private scientific agencies and institutions than to build up an administrative establishment within the government.

In the past half century, the growth of the influence of science has been a distinctive feature of American politics. This has led to developments that seem confusing to those, like the British, who expect consistency in policy. Why, for example, did President Nixon, commonly expected to grasp for more power and influence, choose to abolish his staff agency made up of eminent scientists, which his predecessors had so sedulously sought to build up? Why did Congress enact a law that required the Food and Drug Administration, on the basis of scientific tests, to prohibit the sale of saccharin and then another law to prohibit the prohibition? Why did President Carter set up in his Executive Office one interagency committee, the Regulatory Council, to promote regulations to protect the environment and another, the Regulatory Analysis Review Group, to check those regulations? And why does Congress, which has some thirty thousand staff members on its own payroll, enact laws demanding answers to policy questions from a private agency supported mainly by federal funds, the National Academy of Sciences? If we would look back in American history and ask how such habits developed, we might be able better to appraise how much the lack of discipline and coherence in politics results from Constitutional structure and how much from more fundamental habits of thought or traditional political attitudes.

One such set of attitudes is the habit of active political dissent that prevails today in American scientific institutions, public as well as private, which is accepted as proper by political and administrative authority. It is interesting and significant to note the similarities between these political attitudes and those of the religious dissenters who set the original tone of American politics two or three centuries ago.

Quite different purposes may be embodied in institutions that are similar in their patterns of organization and their relation to political authority. No matter how much churches and scientific institutions may differ from each other, one may well ask the same questions about their relation to politics: how much do they look to the state for support, or take orders from it, and how much do they try to influence what the state does, either by helping decide specific issues or by supplying the general philosophy that justifies its exercise of power?

If one asks such questions about the experience of various countries, curious parallels come up in the answers. The Soviet Academy of Sciences, in its complete dependence on government authority and support and its dedication to a quasi-scientific ideology that justifies absolute authority, is rather like the old Russian Orthodox church in its relation to the czars. At the other extreme the U.S. has a chaotic array of universities, scientific societies, think tanks, environmental action groups, hospitals, and ecological consulting firms. All of these institutions, with respect to their refusal to admit subservience to political authority and their intention to advocate high morality, truth, and good works, resemble the collection of churches, missionary societies, moral reform groups, and utopian communities that once dominated the American social scene and are still today more influential than liberal rationalists like to admit.

If there are interesting similarities or contrasts between the U.S. and the U.K. with respect to the influence of religious and scientific institutions on their politics, they may be worth tracing. This does not mean that such influence has been the only cause, or even the main cause, of the differences in the governmental systems of the two countries. A great many legal, economic, geographic, and sociological factors have come into the picture—a small island at the center of a worldwide empire, dominated until the Second World War by a single ethnic group and a traditional class system, cannot be compared in any simplistic way with a continental power, developed in a disorderly way along an expanding frontier by an amalgam of races and religions. If we are warranted in giving attention to the historical influence of religious and scientific institutions on our respective political systems, it is because the particular influence has been so unfashionable as a subject of scholarly inquiry in recent years, in view of our preoccupation with the systematic and quantifiable social sciences.

Such an inquiry, it may be important to emphasize, will have little or nothing to do with the essence of religious faith or scientific truth. Both have often been corrupted by their devotees' desire for money or political influence or by the necessity of pursuing their ideal goals in an imperfect world and have thereby accounted for some of the more interesting questions in political theory. But the ways in which the ideas of ecclesiastics and scientists have influenced the political systems of the U.S. and the U.K. may help explain the difference that we too often attribute, rather mechanically, to formal Constitutional structure.

Even if we conclude, as I do, that we do not need to adopt a parliamentary cabinet system by Constitutional amendment, we may still profit by imitating the British in several ways that may be not only more feasible but much more relevant. The first is to understand that precise and specialized forms of knowledge are often an incomplete guide to messy practical problems. The second is that it is easy to become too legalistic and that unduly detailed Constitutional or statutory rules may detract from political responsibility. And the third is that moral certainty is dangerous and moral dilemmas abundant in the conduct of public affairs. These were—at any rate until recent years—attitudes that distinguished British politicians at their best from the more scientistic, legalistic, and reformist approach of American politics.

In order to dig deeper into this subject, let us consider in the following six chapters these questions:

—how the ideas of religious dissenters, which later became incorporated in the political attitudes of scientists, determined the characteristic American approach to legal and political authority on a basis quite different from that of Great Britain;

—how that approach made American radicalism, unlike that of Europe, work toward decentralization of power by emphasizing specialized practical concerns rather than general policy, legalistic controls rather than discretionary authority, and moralistic principles rather than political compromise;

—how, on the other hand, the U.S. and the U.K., sharing a skepticism about the perfectibility of mankind, have not succumbed to the temptation to make science into the basis of a new religion and a new form of tyranny;

—how the early American distaste for any ecclesiastical establishment evolved in later years, with the support of scientists, into governmental systems of personnel, finance, and organization that kept politics open to widespread popular participation, but at the cost of incoherence in policy and irresponsibility in legislation and administration;

—how these difficulties manifest themselves in especially stubborn ways in the institution of the presidency as the center of political leadership;

—and finally, how more effective leadership and a tighter system of accountability might be developed in America if we were to recognize that we cannot deal with such fundamental problems by legalistic changes in the formal Constitution but only by a political consensus to amend our unwritten constitution.

The issues here are too broad to be dealt with by the precise methods of the scientific study of politics and society, but the stakes are high enough to discourage professional timidity.

I

Saints and Scientists

After the American and French revolutions, hereditary dynasties began to lose their power throughout the western world. The radical movements that replaced them were avowedly egalitarian in their purposes. But it is curious that in this democratic movement the United States was unique in at least one way. Everywhere else, from the mild Whig reforms in Great Britain to the Bolshevik terror in Russia, the result was to strengthen the administrative centralization of the state. The remnants of feudal independence in the provinces and of autonomy in the guilds and bureaucratic corporations gave way to political centralization and consolidated management.

In the United States, however, the current of revolutionary democracy ran in the opposite direction. The attitudes of religious dissenters in the eighteenth century were absorbed into the thinking of scientists in the nineteenth. Indeed, just before and after the American Revolution the dissenting theologians and the scientists were often the same persons or at least were parts of a common culture; it was only later that science and religion came into conspicuous conflict. In those decisive early years, the social attitudes of both modes of thought were against central authority and settled establishments in church or state.

Thus Hamilton's strong central government lost out to Jeffersonian states' rights, Jefferson's ideas of rule by a natural aristocracy succumbed to the Jacksonian spoils system, and states and cities fragmented their administrative structure by the popular election of many administrative officials. Even after the Civil War, the federal government, which had been saved by its Constitution from such a populist fragmentation of the executive branch, systematically cut down the authority of the President both informally by transferring control of administration to congressional committees and formally by creating boards and commissions, more or less independent of any central control, for major administrative functions.

Thus the United States turned away from the direction in which radical politics was evolving on the continent of Europe. How and why it did so is worth discussion later. We may ask first why it turned away also from the direction of development in Great Britain, which more than a century earlier had had the first of the modern revolutions—the Puritan rebellion that had beheaded the King, abolished the monarchy, and set up under Cromwell a republican Commonwealth over Scotland and Ireland as well as England.[1] Memories of that revolution, which had stimulated the emigration of dissenters to America, were much in the minds of the leaders of the rebellious colonies.

The ideas that produced the Commonwealth were the first effective challenge to the divine right of the dynasties that ruled Europe. In an age when the established church controlled education, supplied the main channel of communication to the people, and produced the clerks and chancellors who managed the King's business, the structure of the ecclesiastical establishment and the beliefs on which it rested were the key issues in public administration. The English church was itself a monarchy, with the King as its head. The principles on which it was established were a formidable support to the King's civil authority—the apostolic succession of the bishops, making impossible the control of congregations by their members; the bishops' subordination not to the pope but to the King as the head of the English church; their control of the instruments of salvation, the sacraments; and their merger with political power as members of the House of Lords. As King James I summed it up so neatly, "No Bishop, No King."

John Adams, more than a decade before he was converted to rebellion, saw the connection between the monarchy and the ecclesi-

16

astical establishment, but with less approval. In his *Dissertation on the Canon and Feudal Law*, published in Boston in 1765 and soon after in London, Adams argued that his Puritan ancestors, in order "to render the popular power in their new government as great and wise as their principles of theory," had rejected the ideas of absolution and uninterrupted apostolic succession, and "for this reason, they demolished the whole system of diocesan episcopacy" and rejected "the divine, miraculous original of government, with which the priesthood had enveloped the feudal monarch in clouds and mysteries. . . . They knew that government was a plain, simple, intelligible thing, founded in nature and reason, and quite comprehensible by common sense."[2] This was more than a half century ahead of Andrew Jackson.

The fundamental ideas on which this political radicalism was based came from religion. John Calvin had argued that man did not depend on the church as an organization to authenticate Scripture, which is instead "confirmed by the internal testimony of the spirit."[3] The doctrines of the depravity of all mankind (including kings and priests) and of the priesthood of all believers were the bases of egalitarian attitudes toward politics as well as religion. Moreover, they separated the basis of civil political authority from that of religion; the faithful were obliged to honor their legal duties to civil magistrates regardless of their religion, while even the magistrate who professed true faith could not deny the right of ordinary laymen to make for themselves the most important decisions affecting their beliefs and their lives.

The established church—Anglican as well as Roman—held that human understanding is so fallible that the laity must rely on the institutional authority of the church. The early Puritans disagreed. Their doctrine of justification by faith was tied to their conviction that every believer must read and interpret Scripture for himself. The most zealous Puritans—Congregationalists in New England and Independents of various sects in the old country—were bitterly intolerant, but their doctrines made it impossible to establish a comprehensive and continuous authority. The distinction between the order of divine grace, under which each believer could appeal directly to God without regard to any human authority, and the order of law or nature, which had to be enforced by political methods, justified the dissenting congregations in giving up the effort to enforce uniformity of belief that had obsessed Calvin's Geneva and the original settlers of Massachusetts Bay. The law of the state was not to define what was right, but to maintain individual rights.

Under pressure from the Levellers in England, and the Baptists in Rhode Island, the right of free religious dissent came to be accepted as a political principle. It would be many years before it would take full effect, even in America. But in the mid-eighteenth century the toleration of dissent and the separation of church and state came to be affirmed not only by the tolerant skeptic but by the most fervent evangelists: Jonathan Edwards rejected the idea of the Holy Commonwealth of New England, and preached that since the church must be "gathered out of the world" the union of the church and the town meeting had to be broken.[4]

The tradition of religious dissent contained the seeds not only of political dissent but also of universal suffrage. The agitators in Cromwell's army had debated the issue in 1648. As one of them said, "There is no person that is under a just government . . . unless he by his free consent be put under that government . . . and therefore . . . there is never a person in England but ought to have a voice in electing; there are no laws that in the strictness and vigour of justice any man is bound to that are not made by those whom he doth consent to."[5]

Universal suffrage was too much for Cromwell, but he held firmly to some older constitutional ideas that were to be taken up later in America. As he lectured his Parliament in 1654: "In every Government there must be Somewhat Fundamental, Somewhat like a *Magna Charta*, which should be standing, be unalterable. . . . That Parliaments should not make themselves perpetual is a Fundamental. . . . Again, is not Liberty of Conscience in Religion a Fundamental? . . . Liberty of Conscience is a natural right; and he that would have it, ought to give it; . . . Every Sect saith: 'Oh! give me liberty!' But give it him, and to his power he will not yield it to anybody else."[6] The instrument of government was Cromwell's fundamental law, the Commonwealth's effort to provide a written and fixed constitution. It provided for the protection of individual rights and for the separation of governmental powers among an executive, a parliament, and a council, which served as a check on the executive during the intervals between parliamentary sessions.

After the death of Cromwell and the restoration of the Stuart line, these constitutional ideas were firmly rejected. The Commonwealth was an unhappy memory because of the fanaticism and instability of government that had been associated with it. When James II seemed likely to threaten the stability of the kingdom again, especially by his moves toward association with the Roman church, the nation reacted once more against the idea of divine right, but more cautiously. The Glorious Revolution of 1689, bringing William of Orange and Mary jointly to the throne and guaranteeing the Protestant succession, set England again on the road away from arbitrary royal authority but not by the route of a constitution that would establish a separation of powers.

The purpose was still to reject the Jacobite succession (*i.e.*, the old Stuart dynasty, with its pretensions to divine right) in order to avoid the danger of popery. But the new approach was quite different from that of the Puritan Commonwealth, which had tried to be a republic with a written constitution. The kingdoms of England and Scotland were consolidated into a new Great Britain with a single Parliament in 1707, and in 1715 the Hanoverian dynasty was brought to the throne with King George I, who was unlikely to assert personal power, being unable to speak English with his ministers. The new approach was to combine the episcopal ecclesiastical establishment with the unlimited legal authority, not of the Parliament alone, but of the King in Parliament.

There was some trouble with Scotland. The Scots had not liked the formula by which the English Parliament had got rid of their King James VII (in England, James II). The English, who did not want to encourage the idea that a parliament could again depose a King, took the position that James had abdicated; the Scottish Convention Parliament resolved that James had not only sought to undermine the Protestant faith but had also "attacked the fundamental constitutions of this [the Scottish] Kingdom, and altered it from a legal limited monarchy, to an arbitrary despotic power." In 1704 the Scottish Parliament enacted a statute that on the death of Queen Anne her successor was not to be the same as the heir to the crown of England unless there were legal guarantees securing the religion, political independence, and trade of Scotland. But these efforts to avoid merger into a system which put unlimited authority in the King in Parliament in Westminster were fruitless after the Act of Union of 1707.[7]

The intermarriage of the great families of England and Scotland, the merger of their commercial interests, and the common fear of a Jacobite restoration and of popery—all these forces consolidated the power of the political leaders who controlled the government in the era when the Cabinet system was slowly developing. That system had an element of stability that was lacking in other countries that later imitated it, relying on structural devices like votes of no confidence and dissolution of the legislature. "The King in Parliament" was a phrase with a more subtle significance. It meant that the Parliament could have authority only if it accepted the essential substance of monarchical government, which at first depended on an established church and in the nineteenth century slowly came to depend on a powerful civil service establishment. It was these foundations of the monarchy, rather than the structural formula of party responsibility, that gave the British system its coherence and authority.

There were still in the eighteenth century a few dissenters against this system who called themselves the Real Whigs and based their ideas on those of the Puritan Commonwealth. They wanted disestablishment of the church; a federal system to restore autonomy to Scotland and Ireland; a separation of the legislative and executive powers to check the omnipotence of Parliament and its dominance by the Prime Minister's patronage; nonpartisan and moralistic politics; and not only freedom of religious opinion but the right of dissenters to hold public office. These "Commonwealthmen"—most of them dissenters in religion—admired the writings of John Milton, James Harrington, Algernon Sidney, and other philosophic defenders of the Puritan experiment with republicanism, but the main currents of English political thought in the eighteenth century were against them.[8]

The ideas of the Commonwealthmen were to bear fruit, not in

their home country, but in America. The similarity between the ideas of the "Honest Whigs" and the leaders of the American Revolution was a striking one: both founded their political philosophy on a union of religious dissent and faith in the new science of the era. Some of the most eminent English dissenters saw the New World as the best opportunity for the development of their ideas. Among the most influential of them was Thomas Hollis, a wealthy English dissenter whom Samuel Johnson blamed for the American Revolution.[9] Hollis was a one-man philanthropic foundation: he bought books on political liberty for distribution to a half-dozen European countries as well as to the American colonies. He had John Adams' *Dissertation on the Canon and Feudal Law* republished in London and gave a considerable library collection of political and scientific works to Harvard College.

Hollis was a member of an eminent Baptist family that personified the eighteenth-century drift from rigorous Calvinist dissent to the scientific Enlightenment. Two generations earlier, another Thomas Hollis, a republican Whig and a zealous devotee of commonwealth principles, had justified his ideas by appealing to sixteenth-century Huguenot writings, which in turn had based theories of popular sovereignty and federalism on Calvin's teachings.[10] He not only began the family habit of distributing propaganda for republican ideas but endowed two professorships at Harvard, one in divinity and one in "natural philosophy," which are still awarded to eminent theologians and physicists.[11]

Hollis' combination of divinity with "natural philosophy," or physics, among his interests was not unusual among eighteenth-century intellectuals or their predecessors. Science had developed in the seventeenth century in England mainly among the dissenters. Charles Webster has described the ways in which the ideas summed up in Francis Bacon's *Great Instauration* were allied with early Puritanism—the scientific idea of progress was based in its early years on the faith of the Puritans that the revolution would lead to the millennium, "the time appointed for the restitution of man's dominance over nature." And Robert K. Merton has given the classic account of how the philosophical orientation and social connections of the seventeenth-century Puritans led to the flowering of science. They dominated its institutional support even after the Restoration in 1660 of King Charles II, who granted the charter of the new Royal Society, the first English equivalent of the scientific academies on the Continent.[12]

For more than a century thereafter, it was not in the institutions of the Anglican establishment but among the dissenters that science flourished. Isaac Newton combined mystical religious beliefs of an idiosyncratic nature with his revolutionary scientific theories. In relation to Christian theology, he was an Arian or Unitarian, and he had to conceal such ideas in order to hold the position in the Church of England on which his Cambridge University status depended. Cambridge and Oxford universities, the heart of the Anglican establishment, remained closed to dissenters and intolerant of science for the next century. The advancement of science in Britain depended on the learned societies, the dissenting academies, and the Scottish universities.[13]

Most members of the Royal Society in the eighteenth century, like Newton, were willing to keep their political and ecclesiastical opinions quiet in order to enjoy royal patronage, much as the dissenting churches refrained from opposing the Hanoverian dynasty, which they believed to be their best protection against a Stuart restoration. Bonnie Prince Charles was all too likely, they feared, to encourage popery. But a few scientists of note were active among those who persisted in their devotion to the constitutional ideas of the old Commonwealth. By the time of the American Revolution, the two most notable were Joseph Priestley and Richard Price, who both incurred the wrath of Edmund Burke for their advanced political ideas. Priestley's *Essay on the First Principles of Government* and Price's *Observations on the Nature of Civil Liberty* were typical of the coterie that called themselves the Honest Whigs, which Benjamin Franklin joined in their fortnightly meetings at the London Tavern.[14]

Priestley, the discoverer of oxygen (although his persistent belief in phlogiston, the supposed essence of combustibility, kept him from understanding what he had discovered), was a Unitarian in religion and a staunch defender of the French Revolution. After a mob supporting "Church and King" destroyed his home, he emigrated to

America in 1791, where he retired to a small Pennsylvania town and cultivated his connections with the American Philosophical Society, which Benjamin Franklin had founded as America's equivalent of the Royal Society.[15]

Richard Price was a particularly significant combination of religious and scientific thought, and his political principles, which drew a special denunciation from Burke, were sympathetic to the rise of republican revolutions through Europe as well as America. A doctor of divinity and a fellow of the Royal Society, a Unitarian in faith and a statistician as well as a preacher by profession, he did the calculations on which was founded the first mutual life insurance society in England and was invited by the Continental Congress in 1778 to come to America as its financial adviser.[16] In his political and constitutional as well as his religious views, he was a dissenter from the mainstream of British thought. He supported the American cause in 1776, arguing that the cause of civil liberty required a federal system, limits on parliamentary omnipotence, and a system of representation in which each area elected its own members of a parliament with taxing powers.[17] These heresies were enough to explain Burke's denunciation of his approach to politics: "the age of chivalry is gone. That of sophisters, economists, and calculators, has succeeded; and the glory of Europe is extinguished for ever."[18]

By this time, the two streams of constitutional thought—British and American—had separated. Both were to move toward greater freedom and democratic rule but by different institutional forms. The British formula was the doctrine of virtual representation and the unlimited supremacy of the King in Parliament: it did not matter that a particular local constituency had no representative of its own in Parliament as long as the same class was represented. The Americans were appealing to an older doctrine, the right of each local community to have its own delegate to the legislature, and the subordination of that legislature to a fundamental law.[19]

Both countries distrusted the unlimited authority of legislative bodies, but America sought to constrain that authority by legalistic institutions—a constitution to be interpreted by an independent judiciary—while the British constrained it even more effectively by associating the elective house with a monarchy and an establishment. The establishment in the late eighteenth century was still the Church of England, but over the years it came to share influence with its lay successor, the established civil service. The ministers of the Crown cannot govern today without the support of a majority of the elected house. But they rise to power only after serving their apprenticeship in the Commons, accepting the historic obligations and loyalty expected of those who are for life "sworn of the Privy Council," and learning to respect the integrity and continuity of H.M. Civil Service, the administrative embodiment of the monarchy. This is a very different system from the model in the minds of those who, following Harold Laski's simplification of Walter Bagehot, think of the Cabinet as little more than the executive committee of an all-powerful unicameral national assembly.[20]

The American political creed, by the time of the Revolution, was already firmly set in a different direction by ideas like those derived from the seventeenth-century Puritan Commonwealth, which—like the ideas of Joseph Priestley and Richard Price—seemed fully compatible with those of the eighteenth-century Enlightenment and the new science. That fusion was encouraged by the fact that the eighteenth-century heirs of the old religious tradition were more interested in the new science than were their nineteenth- (and some of their twentieth-) century successors, and the leaders of the new science retained much sympathy, for all their skepticism, with religious ideals.

The political compatibility of these two currents of thought was typified in the presidential election of 1800 between John Adams and Thomas Jefferson, the two men who in private life headed the country's two main scientific societies.

Adams was at the time president of the American Academy of Arts and Sciences. As an heir to the old Calvinist tradition, he was already a Unitarian and an Arminian in theology, having less faith in selection by grace and more in good works than his forebears. And he had enough faith in the new science to have his wife and children submit to the risk of the new smallpox inoculation—from which Jonathan Edwards had died a few years before.[21]

Jefferson was president of the American Philosophical Society, more outspokenly skeptical in theology but with strong religious interests—the only American President to edit an abridged New Testament to his own tastes, omitting supernatural references and emphasizing moral teachings.[22] He always affirmed his political allegiance to the ideas of Bacon, Newton, and Locke, and his scientific interests ranged from paleontology—in which he tried to disprove the theory of Buffon, the French naturalist, that animals in the New World were naturally inferior—to psychology—in which he tried to explore the material basis of the mental faculties. The fusion of his religious and scientific ideas found their aesthetic expression in his interest in classical law and philosophy and in Palladian architecture, as in his beloved Monticello.[23] In this way he was typical of many eighteenth-century political leaders and students of government, from both the religious and the scientific strains of thought, who were inclined to find common ground by exploring the experience of the classical republics of Greece and Rome.

During this transitional period between the colonial era and the onset of Jacksonian democracy, religion and science were exceptionally compatible in their attitudes to politics, for two reasons.

First, in their outlook on science, the leading Puritan theologians of the eighteenth century had more sympathy and understanding than did their nineteenth-century successors. Cotton Mather, for example, was elected to the Royal Society for his success with inoculation for smallpox and his experiments with plant genetics. And more Americans were elected to the Royal Society during the eighteenth century than the nineteenth.[24]

More fundamentally, the early Calvinists, as Perry Miller observed, had a "perception of the identity of natural order and divine decree."[25] Jonathan Edwards, who had based some of his theological ideas on Newton's scientific discoveries, had no difficulty in accepting the scientific theories of causation and determinism; like others among the more sophisticated theologians, he found it easy to reconcile his views on predestination with the materialistic approach of scientific determinism. He was confident that the coming of the millennium might be hastened by human efforts and was no more bothered by the apparent inconsistency between predestination and the exercise of free will than later scientists were between material determinism and their obligation to act in the interest of progress.

And he indeed believed that the spiritual contemplation of the saints during the millennium would be encouraged by the "contrivances and inventions" that were being developed to free them from secular cares and to enable them to assist "one another through the whole earth by more expedite, easy, and safe communication between distant regions than now."[26]

Newton had found it possible to explain the workings of the solar system by insisting that he could calculate how the planets moved around the sun and could measure the force of gravitation and thereby predict their movements but that it was not necessary to say why they moved as they did or what gravity really was. By renouncing any public interest in the purpose of scientific laws (in philosophic terms, renouncing the teleology that had dominated science since Aristotle) and reducing science to the consideration of causes and effects, Newton, even though he was an Arian or Unitarian in theology, made it easier for the rigorous Calvinists like Edwards to accept his approach.[27] Edwards, indeed, went so far as to accept the idea of a "material world" which obeyed "the laws of motion, and the course of nature" so steadily that it might theoretically be predicted to the end of time by some "very able mathematician."[28]

Second, in the relation of religion to politics, it was the evangelistic and conservative theologians, not the enlightened skeptics, who were the more radical revolutionaries. Patrick Henry and Samuel Adams were earlier and stronger in taking up the cause of independence than their more genteel and intellectual compatriots. The Great Awakening, the religious revival of the 1740s of which Jonathan Edwards was the leading figure, was a greater stimulus to political radicalism than was the intellectual skepticism of the Unitarian movement in Boston. Indeed, revolutionary pamphleteers explicitly argued for unrestrained rule by the popular majority on the basis of the belief in the total depravity of mankind as taught by Edwards.[29]

In the early eighteenth century, the Church of England, through its Society for the Propagation of the Gospel, began to make an effort to build up the Anglican establishment in the colonies. Even in Puritan New England, churches were set up under episcopal rule. The only substantial Anglican establishment was in Virginia, which was rapidly becoming indifferent if not deist in religion, but the Anglicans took the lead in establishing the educational institutions that were to become Columbia University and the University of Pennsylvania and in stimulating such missionary work as that of the Wesleys and George Whitefield, whose preaching made such a great impact on the colonies from Georgia northward to New England.

These efforts were resented by the great majority of the religious sects throughout the colonies, whose diversity made them all suspicious of any effort to extend the Anglican establishment. Indeed, the Puritans and many dissenters were against the Stamp Act especially because it seemed to pave the financial way for the introduction of episcopacy into New England. While both England and America had great religious revivals in the mid-eighteenth century it was politically significant that their leaders in America were Calvinists, while in England they were Methodists, remaining Anglican and Episcopal in relation to the national establishment while becoming more rigorous in moral standards.

After the success of the American Revolution, the more popular and evangelistic churches continued to be the more radical influences in politics. But radicalism then had little to do with issues as they would come to be defined in nineteenth-century Europe or twentieth-century America. Radicalism meant opposition to any establishment, whether ecclesiastical or governmental. On this basis, the Baptists and other popular sects—conservative in their theology but not in their politics—could comfortably side with Jefferson against the Federalists, fearing his Deism less than any establishment of religion, even one set up on Congregational rather than Episcopal lines.[30]

The upper-class intellectual leadership of New England, Federalist in its politics, was slow to give up the idea of a religious establishment, once there was no longer any danger of its being constituted on an episcopal basis, that is, under a centralized hierarchy governed by appointed bishops. For example, William Ellery Channing, the intellectual leader of the Unitarian movement, was still arguing in 1820 that "government is throughout a moral and religious institution" and that Christianity "perfectly coincides with government in its spirit and ends," so that the establishment of religion and its support by tax funds—but allowing each citizen to select "the particular form of christianity to which he will give support"—was justified.[31] But the Massachusetts establishment of religion was finally abolished by law in 1833 after gradually being given up in practice by the townships, and the result was vastly to strengthen the competing sects of enthusiasts against the more rationalist Unitarians.[32]

Jefferson's politics had defeated his theology. He had believed that Unitarianism would soon become the leading American religion. Aside from its temporary reliance on a highly local kind of establishment, its doctrine and principles were in accord with Jefferson's faith in rational thought, dislike of the Calvinist belief in human depravity, and confidence in progress. While the Unitarians professed no formal creed, their beliefs were summed up in the affirmation of faith drafted after Jefferson's time by James Freeman Clarke, Professor of Natural Religion and Christian Doctrine at the Harvard Divinity School: "I believe in the Fatherhood of God, the Brotherhood of Man, the Leadership of Jesus, Salvation by Character, and the Progress of Mankind onward and upward forever."[33]

Such an informal creed, however congenial it would have been to Jefferson, was too intellectual to withstand the emotional and doctrinaire appeal of nineteenth-century evangelism. Something like it had indeed prospered for a time even in the South, where Unitarians briefly headed Transylvania College in Kentucky, the first college west of the Appalachians, and later the College of South Carolina.[34] But the movement sagged under the pressure of the Calvinists, especially the Presbyterians and Baptists, who looked on Unitarian doctrine as entirely too tolerant, with respect not only to its theology but also to issues of personal behavior and politics.

The practical politics of the Jeffersonian era, and even more of the Jacksonian, owed much less to the intellectual teachings of the French Enlightenment than to the emotional and moralistic radicalism of the evangelical camp meeting. The southern states were especially influenced by the great wave of religious revivals at the turn of the century (as intense if not as intellectual as those of the Great Awakening of the mid-eighteenth century) that culminated in 1801 in the great Cane Ridge camp meetings in Kentucky. These revivals expressed the demand of populist leaders for churches founded on egalitarian political principles, renouncing not only any official establishment but also any form of governing organization and any system of education for the clergy—"a church without organization and a theology without theory," as one historian has summed up their goals. This general approach led to the 1794 secession of the "Republican Methodists" in Virginia from the episcopal system of the orthodox Methodists and to the departure from the Presbyterian churches in Kentucky of the leaders of the Cane Ridge camp meetings, and in Pennsylvania of Alexander Campbell and his associates in the Disciples of Christ.[35]

In their emphasis on individualism in religious experience, these movements worked not only against governmental establishments and church organization but even against family and community: the denominations that profited most from the camp meeting disapproved of infant baptism and insisted on a direct personal commitment before admitting a communicant. The conditions of life on the frontier encouraged such strong individualism: even the Whiskey Rebellion, in which the farmers of western Pennsylvania protested the efforts of the federal government to tax the output of their backwoods stills, was justified by evangelical doctrine and led to the migration of many fervently religious families westward to the less oppressed counties of Kentucky.[36]

The westward migrants from New England showed more interesting intellectual variety in their populist theologies. The religious zeal of the eighteenth-century Puritan became transmuted in the first half of the nineteenth century in Vermont and upper New York state into a great variety of perfectionist sects, many the result of the desire of religious liberals to find a pseudoscientific dogma. This was the hotbed of the early prohibition movement, phrenology, mesmerism, premillennialism, spiritualism, Mormonism, and such antinomian sects as the Oneida Community. (That community's early experiments with free love did not survive the bitter criticism of its neighbors, and it settled down later on into a highly prosperous manufacturing establishment.)[37]

The major Protestant churches, by contrast, were responding to the leadership of the revivalist preachers, such as Charles Grandison Finney, who were no longer interested in theological doctrine but were demanding the individual exercise of free will to lead to salvation. This was the approach that seemed to offer the most promise for dealing with the social problems of the rapidly growing urban centers, and it encouraged the creation of temperance societies and YMCAs throughout the country. The evangelists with the greatest popular appeal were uninterested in the theological ideas of the churches with the most highly educated clergy—the Episcopalians, Unitarians, and Presbyterians—and tended to believe that religion should be relied on to sustain the nation in the absence of strong political authority. As Perry Miller observed, nineteenth-century evangelism "might almost be called a conspiracy to obliterate the original dedication to a highly intellectual system of theology."[38]

By the middle of the nineteenth century, there was no longer any threat in America of a religious establishment based on a conservative theology. The separation of church and state was taken for granted. As new ethnic and religious groups migrated from Europe, they no longer were governed in their choice of political affiliations by the doctrines of their churches. The Calvinists had based their dissenting political attitudes on a hatred of the political authoritarianism that was supported by popery, and Jefferson was as ardent as any Puritan in seeking to break the connection between priestly doctrines and practical politics. Yet by 1831, Tocqueville, while acknowledging that the American Revolution had been effected by "men who, after having shaken off the authority of the Pope . . . brought with them into the New World a form of Christianity which I cannot better describe than by styling it a democratic and republican religion," nevertheless argued that the Irish Catholic immigrants "constitute the most republican and the most democratic class of citizens which exists in the United States. . . . They constitute a minority, and all rights must be respected in order to insure to them the free exercise of their own privileges."[39]

The later waves of immigration brought to America other ethnic and religious groups that were glad to escape from orthodox religions and political authority and eager to be accepted into a secular society that would tolerate or respect differences of religious opinion, and irreligious opinion as well. The Protestants of northern and western Europe, the Catholics and Orthodox from the south and east, and the Jews from the German states, the Balkans, and Russia were all to join later in the nineteenth and in the twentieth century in the political amalgam of America and to share in its civil religion.

As they did so, they generally accepted the basic constitutional and political ideas that had been developed by the era of the Enlightenment, in which the older Puritan attitudes were being transmuted slowly into those congenial to modern science. And they even took for granted those political ideas as they were popularized by the social conditions of the frontier into a generally antigovernment ethos and a preference for weak executive institutions and general fragmentation of authority.

As the churches split into many competing denominations, all concerned mainly with social action or the psychological welfare of their individual members, and as science came to be justified by the technological progress accomplished by private industry, there came to be less and less reason for the average citizen to see the government as a whole as a unique source of authority deserving of allegiance and support.[40]

In tracing the evolution of political theories or attitudes, one can never prove a sequence of cause and effect in a scientific manner. Even biologists have enough trouble proving their theories of evolution and have to be content without the test of replicable experiment. In order to understand the difference between British and American political habits and traditions—not only in formal constitutional structure but also in the practical political issues of government organization and coordination of policy—we need to understand how they have been determined by the curiously similar attitudes of the early religious dissenters and contemporary scientists.

This requires no original discovery: the main outlines of the influence of early Calvinism on American political development were sketched out by George Bancroft a century ago in terms that are unfashionable today because they sound like small-town Fourth of July oratory more than careful scholarship. More recently, theological writers have developed the point at a more theoretical level—for example, Ernst Troeltsch in Germany before the First World War, and H. Richard Niebuhr in America.[41] In the United States, in our imperative need to reduce political prejudice against religious minorities, we may have tried to forget the active political role of religious groups and the bitter quarrels among them. As society became more and more secularized, more and more faith came to be placed in science rather than dogma as the key to human salvation. This change in faith led many scholarly and ambitious intellects to turn for a vocation from the ministry to science. The sons of ministers elected scientific careers, and in America the denominational (especially Congregational) colleges produced disproportionate numbers of leading scientists.[42]

Meanwhile, scholars have continued to admire the studies that give credit (or blame) to Calvinism for the growth of capitalism, especially those of Max Weber and R. H. Tawney.[43] The interpretation of Michael Walzer, who sees that influence as later and less direct than the political influence of early Calvinism on the Puritan revolution of the seventeenth century and on subsequent radicalism, seems more warranted by the evidence, and more apt as an explanation for later political developments in both England and America.[44]

We need in any case not only to try to interpret abstract doctrine but to observe the way groups of people—in this case, early religious dissenters and later scientists—behave in practice in their relation to government and politics. The transition from the earlier to the later group came about gradually. Whatever the influence of their specific beliefs, the dissenting clergy and the later scientists were similar in their temperamental preference for types of vocation. Neither profession was the route to wealth or political power. Both tended to appeal to those who would not have felt comfortable in political campaigns or managerial responsibility and whose intellectual interests dedicated them to abstract ideas and discouraged pragmatic compromise.[45]

Faith is the substance of things hoped for and not necessarily a matter of literal and confident conviction. In that sense, as the more scholarly intellects turned to science rather than religion as a vocation, they were reflecting a major shift in the faith of the more deeply concerned and highly educated citizens. The old belief in the millennium—the era of a thousand years of felicity that was to occur either just before or just after the Second Coming of Christ and the General Judgment—gave way to a belief in the perpetual progress of mankind, for which science would provide the driving force.

As this change occurred, the scientists were faced with issues about their relationship to political and administrative authority to which they responded in ways reminiscent of their predecessors among the religious dissenters. It may now be interesting to see how the earlier attitudes of the dissenters became established in the political habits of modern scientists.

II

The Dissenting Establishment

No one can measure with any confidence how much a political movement is affected by abstract ideals and how much by material interests. In a cynical era it is tempting to dismiss the ideals completely and to explain everything by economic or other materialistic causes. But then there is the danger that materialism itself will become a philosophic dogma, supported by a new kind of uncritical faith.

With respect to one's own personal motivations in matters of religion, who can tell how much one is influenced by pure faith and how much by conventionality, by yearning for psychological comfort, or by the need to be sustained in competitive professional endeavor? Similarly, in affairs of science, what scholar can say how much he is driven by a zeal for pure knowledge and how much by competitive pride, desire for promotion, or hopes for a prize? It must be far more difficult to judge how deeply a nation is moved by abstract ideals and how much by material interests.

As easy as it is to distrust one's own motives, it is much more agreeable to distrust others. One may be confirmed in this distrust either by the Calvinist doctrine of the total depravity of mankind, especially of the rich and of the rulers, or by various modern scientific theories which ascribe our pretensions of civic virtue to subconscious economic or psychological motives. We may, however, be inclined today to give too little credit to the unselfish or idealistic purposes that are occasionally mixed in with our normal political corruption.

We cannot, of course, be precise in such matters. But it does seem clear that the American Revolution was guided by a small number of intellectual leaders with not only economic and materialistic motives but also a new set of political ideals. These ideals were derived not only from the obvious sources in legal and political theory but also in part from the concepts of religious dissent and in part from the nascent scientific ideals of the Enlightenment.

Obviously many other motives were at work: sectional interests, ethnic conflicts, trade rivalries, and other forms of organized selfishness. Indeed, as soon as national independence was assured and the westward expansion began, the idealistic motives were submerged in the populist land-grabbing and money-grubbing attitudes that drew the scorn of European visitors imbued with the genteel aristocratic tradition. One may even suppose that the separation of church and state, while it protected religion from political control, also made it impossible for the state to use religion to enforce a modicum of good order and dignity and restraint on competing economic interests.

The earlier theological metaphor for this competition between the abstract ideal and pragmatic materialism was the issue whether one is justified by faith or by works. The doctrine of justification by faith, which Calvin developed from the theology of Saint Augustine, provided a rationale for freeing the churches from the domination of government; from the point of view of the believer, there could be no practical test of his prospects of salvation and hence no excuse for government to try to control the details of religious belief. The opposite Arminian doctrine of justification by works involved the church in relations with government. If salvation came through works, the government, being concerned with conduct and morals, therefore felt required to maintain an ecclesiastical establishment.

In a roughly analogous way, the scientist's dedication to the pursuit of truth requires freedom from political constraints, while a dedication to the justification of science in society by its good works—the benefits attained by practical applications in such matters as health, industrial progress, or military power—obviously involves a continuous interaction with political processes.

The institutions of religion and of science differ widely in their methods of thought and their approach to truth. But with respect to their relation to political power, both must develop some accommodation. The terms on which that relationship is developed are significant to the nature of the state, not only in philosophical theory but also in practical politics and the details of administrative organization and procedure. For if either religion or science is justified by its works, it is important to know whether it is under the control of the state—that is, of the central authority of government—or is left free to operate under a variety of independent institutions. A truly effective establishment, either of religion or science, can be maintained only by some centralized hierarchical structure.

Let us put off any specific discussion of those pragmatic issues until Chapter IV and in this chapter consider the ways in which the political attitudes of modern scientists are related to those of the old religious dissenters. The resemblance seems especially significant in three main ways, all of which have to do with the effectiveness of government and even more with its responsibility to the people. These ways are:

The Relation of Abstract Thought to Practical Concerns

The scientific community, like the old ecclesiastical leadership, professes a pure faith in basic knowledge. To get public support, however, it must show its practical contributions to society. But then it discovers that the more basic approach to truth is actually more effective in attaining practical results, and that undue emphasis on applied results may result in grave social conflict. This is the dilemma of our "policy for science."

The Relation of the Ideal of Direct Democracy to the Rule of Law

Dissenting evangelists believed that every church member should read and interpret the Bible for himself, and similarly, a great variety of scientific or quasi-scientific organizations are committed to educating the general public in scientific truth as it relates to practical concerns. But they both, as they deal with political issues, whether of public morals or the control of technology, tend to assume that the rights and the equality of all citizens must be maintained by public debate and the enactment of laws rather than by discretionary authority. The result may be to reduce the arbitrary power of political leaders but also to reduce the political responsibility of government. This the dilemma of "science for policy."

The Incentives for Political Compromise and
Administrative Coordination

The effect on politics of science, like that of the earlier dissenting theology, has been to check the power of political leaders and prevent the growth of an irresponsible establishment. Against this benefit must be weighed the exaggerated specialization of authorities and functions in government, the danger of giving undue influence in complex issues to experts, and the difficulty of presenting the issues to the public in ways that support a genuine system of accountability. This is the dilemma of the reformer, whose perfectionism may sometimes lead to worse results than does the arrogance of the demagogue or the bureaucrat.

Let us take these three points up in turn, and pay special attention to the ways they reenforce one another.

Abstract Thought and Practical Applications

Before the American Revolution, the New England Puritans had recognized the conflict between their abstract theological belief and its practical results; a similar conflict has been recurrent in both religion and science and persists today. Max Weber argued in the twentieth century that, in economic issues, the Protestant ethic contributed to the spirit of capitalism, which corroded the earlier religious ideals.[1] Cotton Mather had summed up the same process two centuries earlier—in 1700—in the judgment he passed on the Puritans of Plymouth: "Their chief *Hazard* and *Symptom* of *Degeneracy*, is in the Verification of that Old Observation, *Religio peperit Divitias, & Filia devoravit Matrem: Religion* brought forth *Prosperity*, and the *Daughter* destroy'd the *Mother.*"[2]

His predecessors among theological leaders had been rigorous in defending the theory of justification by faith rather than by works. Even though a local congregation, which in most of New England was the same as the town government, might put great pressure on its members to conform to moral discipline, some of the more intellectual theologians disapproved of governmental action that, by requiring "outward compliance," would make true believers into "accomplished hypocrites."[3] Even Calvin had, in some ways, tried to eliminate the authority of the ecclesiastical establishment over personal behavior, especially by reducing the number of sacraments by which the hierarchy could exert a magical control over the credulous laity. Calvin and his followers went even so far as to make marriage a civil contract rather than a sacrament of the church.[4]

This is not to say that most Puritans fully accepted the radical distinction that Jonathan Edwards made between salvation by faith and grace and salvation by works. Among religious believers, most could not be so rigorous in maintaining that distinction. As the Calvinist attitudes of discipline and individual responsibility led to greater material prosperity, the Puritans tended to concern themselves more and more with morals and less with abstract belief; Jonathan Edwards considered that even Cotton Mather's slide in that direction went too far in the direction of the Arminian doctrine of justification by works as well as by faith. A similar change in attitude came as they thought about science: while the intellectual leaders of the Puritans had accepted the new physics of Newton because they saw the understanding of natural law as an aid to piety, their successors tended more and more to think of its practical benefits. But as both theologians and scientists in America came to take more interest in practical benefits, they were under no pressure to submit to the central direction of the government. The doctrines of dissent had made impossible the development of any establishment with central authority.

The new interest in the practical cleared the way for the contribution of Jefferson, who saw the importance of science primarily in practical terms. With his interest in rural society and his distaste for urban mobs, he thought of agriculture as "the queen of the sciences," and in his plans for the University of Virginia, he gave it a primary role, thus setting the precedent for the later land-grant colleges for "Agricultural and Mechanic Arts." Daniel J. Boorstin has suggested that the Puritan emphasis on metaphysics and pure science produced at colleges like Harvard a more advanced type of basic knowledge than came from the universities like Virginia that were tied to the social structure and purposes of the community.[5]

The contrast can hardly be an absolute one. The Puritans, too, saw the utility of science not only as an aid to piety but also as a source of practical benefits. As New England became a commercial urban society, science came to be justified more by its works than by its faith. Seen in terms of moral purposes, science had transmuted its earlier Calvinism into a practical Arminian doctrine; that is to say, it had begun to justify its role in society not by its dedication to abstract truth but by its practical results. This dilution of its original pure purpose, however, was very much like a similar change that had taken place in religious belief. The rigorous Calvinism of the seventeenth century, which sought to remove the saints from the concerns of this world, had given way by the eighteenth to the view that piety would also make us rich and happy. Indeed, as Perry Miller has noted, the acceptance of the new physics by the Puritans was encouraged by its advertisement as an aid not only to piety but also to practical benefits.[6]

The zeal for pure knowledge, whether it took the form of faith in divine revelation or of reliance on materialistic determinism, was too pure to remain untainted by pragmatic concerns. Both religion and science led their practitioners to disciplined and devoted exertions that paid off in practical terms and demanded material support. On the side of science, it was clear even by the time of Tocqueville's visit in the 1830s that Americans were more interested in practical technology than in pure science.[7] And for generations thereafter American scientists complained that funds were not available for the advancement of basic knowledge but only for agriculture and the mechanic arts.

But it is a fallacy perhaps to see this process as one of a recent departure from the primitive pure faith of the early basic scientists. The founders of the Royal Society in 1660 and of the American Philosophical Society in 1744 had both followed Francis Bacon in emphasizing the practical advantages to be derived from the support of science. The temptation to practical applications, or justification by works, was, so to speak, the original sin of science. Through the later nineteenth and into the twentieth century, the dominant

American interest in both religion and science was in good works rather than in abstract ideals. Religious concerns were summed up in such movements as the temperance societies, emancipation, and the social gospel. Popular Protestantism became eager to join across denominational boundaries in a civic religion for social progress. Popular science was thought of in much the same way in terms of the practical inventions like those of Thomas Edison.

In both science and religion, a serious challenge began to develop to this preoccupation with practical applications, especially after the First World War. The destruction of the old European order by that war and the revolutions that followed it made it impossible to have confidence any longer in the idea of automatic progress or in too easy an alliance between a rationalist religion and useful technology.

On the side of religion, neo-orthodox thinkers began to emphasize a more fundamental approach to their theology. Karl Barth in Germany and Switzerland, and Reinhold Niebuhr in the United States, as different as they were on practical political issues, agreed in challenging the advocates of the social gospel—the theologians who saw religion mainly in terms of its humanitarian impulses and benefits—to consider again the fundamental theological issues in ways quite different from the thinking of the misnamed fundamentalists.

In the sciences, a similar emphasis on fundamental or basic research began to develop, at first in private scientific societies and philanthropy. There was no central governmental establishment to block such a change: the dissenters, more than a century before, had seen to that. But now it began to seem clear that the old emphasis on practical application was leading the country into grave social problems and, more surprisingly, that an emphasis on basic research would actually be more effective in the development of new technology.

In the 1920s the National Academy of Sciences and the National Research Council undertook to build up basic science in American universities by imitating German research methods. They chose, however, not to follow the German example of having the state set up separate research institutions, but undertook to concentrate their efforts on the private universities of the country and to set up for their graduate students and faculty an ambitious program of fellow-ships for study abroad. The financial support for these programs came from Andrew Carnegie, bred in the Scottish Calvinist tradition, and from John D. Rockefeller, whose Baptist piety was reenforced by his main philanthropic adviser, Frederick T. Gates, a Baptist minister who was convinced that "science and education are the brain and nervous system of civilization" and who admonished Rockefeller that God would finally judge him according to the way in which he disposed of his wealth.[8]

In the 1930s the newly reorganized Rockefeller Foundation de-cided to shift its emphasis in science from the applied programs for "the welfare of mankind" to more fundamental problems in "the advancement of knowledge," to quote the official slogans of its pro-grams. The new science program of the foundation was headed by Warren Weaver, later to play a key role in the administration of the government's wartime program—the Office of Scientific Research and Development. His purpose was to push a reductionist program, rebuilding the discipline of biology on the foundations of molecular physics and chemistry. Physics and engineering had been blamed by some radical critics for the industrial boom of the 1920s and the succeeding depression, and "psychobiology," to use Weaver's term, was the field of study which offered mankind hope of ultimate con-trol over its own genetic inheritance and vital processes. The Rockefeller Foundation program was influential in supporting the managers of scientific research in the decade before the Second World War in the policy of pushing research support in as fundamental, indeed, as reductionist a direction as possible.[9]

It was the success of these private efforts toward the support of basic research that built up the institutions and trained the leaders who were to direct the fusion of governmental and private institu-tions in the advanced weapons program of the Second World War. The Office of Scientific Research and Development (OSRD), headed by Vannevar Bush, president of the Carnegie Institution of Washing-ton, put universities and private research institutions directly in charge of operating the most advanced programs of weapons devel-opment outside the control of the established hierarchy of the armed services. The success of those efforts—the glamor of atomic weap-

ons, radar, and guided missiles—emboldened Bush and his colleagues at the end of the war to press for a program that would provide big government funds for basic science but leave its control in
private institutions.

The arguments that Bush presented to the President and Congress
in 1945, in their emphasis on the need of the scientist for freedom
to pursue his intellectual interest without political restraint, were
reminiscent in all but literary style of the arguments of a John Milton or a Jonathan Edwards for freedom of conscience. Bush, however, was keenly aware that he was making a pragmatic compromise
between the ideal of pure science independent of political interference (the ideal that had made the leaders of the National Academy
of Sciences, before World War II, adamant in their refusal to ask for
federal funds) and the need for money on a large scale. It was with
some qualms that he chose to ask for government support for basic
science.[10]

In the years after the Bush report, when scientists had established
their freedom to pursue research in the interest of basic knowledge
in the style to which the OSRD had accustomed them, they (much
like their ecclesiastical predecessors) found that there was something of a dilemma between the pure pursuit of truth and the maintenance of official support.

The dissenting theologians all believed in the same God, and often
professed their agreement with each other on the main elements of
their faith. Since, however, they rejected membership in an established church which could ask for adherence without being too fussy
about particular beliefs, it was easy for them to split frequently into
competing denominations, each protesting vigorously that it had the
exact formula of salvation. But then, as the country became more
interested in other than religious issues, the denominations began
to soften the sharp edges of the creeds in order to accommodate the
consciences of present members and attract new ones. Moreover,
their preaching often was directed to purposes of a civic or social
nature or to the support of the economic establishment of the country in order to justify their existence and attract financial support.[11]

In a somewhat similar way, scientists of all disciplines have been
strained by the conflict between their dedication to the ideal of a

unified body of truth and their commitment to various specialized theories or their interests in practical applications. The scientific ideal leads to a search for unifying concepts that cut across disciplinary boundaries. Thus, the more abstract or reductionist concepts of physics have been found to govern chemical reactions, and chemistry in turn comes to explain biological phenomena. Geology and botany then become much less the business of the collection and classification of descriptive data and much more a search for the basic laws by which even social and political phenomena may ultimately be explained.[12]

Auguste Comte had envisioned the steady progress of the sciences, in a reductionist direction, starting with astronomy and physics and ultimately combining the whole spectrum of the social sciences in a determinist and quantitative system that he baptized sociology. The most influential apostle of such ideas in the English-speaking world of the nineteenth century (although he disagreed vigorously with Comte on some issues, as we shall see in the next chapter) was Herbert Spencer, who undertook to apply the doctrine of evolution to the understanding of the basic principles of various fields of knowledge. His *First Principles* in 1862 was followed by a series of major works—*The Principles of Biology* and then *The Principles of Psychology*, *The Principles of Sociology*, and extending his reductionism to its ultimate limits, *The Principles of Ethics*. His successors have been less ambitious, and his reputation is lower today than a century ago, but the ideal of applying a systematic and quantitative methodological approach to unify the disciplines devoted to the study of human behavior became the goal of many scientists early in the twentieth century.

The ideal proved hard to work out in practice. Even in the universities, which are the institutions most deeply dedicated to basic science, the business of research seemed to require, not a unified pattern of organization, but continued specialization and subspecialization. Where research called for combinations of disciplinary approach, the result was usually not to combine two scientific departments but to create a third—a biochemistry department might be set up apart from the biology and chemistry departments, for example. And outside the universities, when scientists chose to associate themselves for scholarly discussion, the original comprehensive American Association for the Advancement of Science, embracing the entire range of scientific knowledge, became less influential than the hundreds of specialized societies.[13]

Such high specialization, however, runs into difficulties when an appeal for support must be made to the lay skeptic. If the pursuit of scientific truth requires the researcher to renounce any concern for purpose, he will have to find some way to demonstrate the relevance of his work to human or social benefit when he asks for money. A lecture criticizing teleology is not a persuasive tactic when asking a governmental or foundation officer for money. So at the university, the scientist who is concerned with practical purposes may prefer to work in a professional school rather than a disciplinary department, since a school of engineering or medicine or even public administration may be able to unite research disciplines with teaching programs that have useful applications.

As long as the government was concerned only with obviously practical and applied science, and the support of pure science was a private responsibility, the split between the two seemed of little practical importance. But when the Second World War proved their all too effective connection, the problem of relating scientific thought to legislative and administrative practice became troublesome.

Direct Democracy and the Rule of Law

The early Puritan dissenters, who believed in salvation by faith rather than works, nevertheless undertook in their communities to prescribe and enforce rigorous rules to govern personal conduct. In an equally paradoxical way, they (and even more their more evangelistic successors) emphasized the priesthood of all believers, with all communicants having an equal right to read and interpret the Bible for themselves, in the hope that this would lead to a greater unity of belief among the faithful, only to find that this democratic approach led to an endless fragmentation of sects and denominations.

It would be comfortable for a modern skeptic to believe that such contradictions cannot develop in a scientific era. Yet it is hard for scientists generally to agree on a strategy, in their relation to public affairs, between two courses of action. One course is to accept the democratic principle of equality among the voters, to try to give the general public the rudiments of a scientific education, and especially to try to persuade it to support the independence and influence of scientific institutions. The other is to select specific issues of interest and to lobby vigorously for legislation to settle those issues correctly and by rigid rules. For the scientist as for the theologian, the conflict between confidence in democratic government and the desire to keep it from making dangerous mistakes has led to confusion in policy and to an overemphasis on legalism in public affairs—through both the legislative and the judicial process. The legalistic approach was apparent by the time of the American Revolution: Edmund Burke remarked on the striking degree of influence of lawyers in the politics of the colonies.[14]

That emphasis on the law and the lawyers may seem inconsistent with the other idealized tradition in early American history—the New England town meeting, long considered the prototype of pure democracy, in which everyone had an equal voice. Even today, in the era when Presidents cannot travel without an entourage of staff, security guards, and press agents, they still occasionally feel compelled to appear at something which they call a town meeting to consult with the voters. The original town meeting was, of course, government by the Puritan congregation and its elders, who were the legal authority in many towns until the disestablishment of the churches in the 1820s and 1830s in Connecticut and Massachusetts.

Puritan theology, in theory, emphasized salvation by faith and grace—the covenant of the New Testament, rather than the Old Testament Covenant elaborated in the Ten Commandments and the other laws of the Torah. Yet to avoid the rule of the Anglican bishops, on the one hand, and, on the other, to avoid the excesses of the Fifth Monarchy men, the Levellers, and other sectarians of the radical antinomian variety, the Puritans had to make a practical choice.[15] In popular theology, they put far more emphasis on the legalism of the Old Testament than did the Anglican clergy; the popularity of Old Testament names like Hezekiah and Obadiah in Cromwell's army and on New England colonial tombstones illustrated that emphasis.

The extreme democracy of the town meeting worked against any established authority, ecclesiastical or civil. Those who sought to escape the authority of an ecclesiastical hierarchy by appealing to the layman's literal reading of the Bible naturally sought to escape from discretionary political authority by relying on detailed legislation. As an alternative to discretionary authority, it seemed desirable to emphasize the rule of law—emphasis on legislative and judicial process rather than on unified political authority or centralized administrative discipline. Vestiges of that tradition in New England still hold weight today: the city manager movement, which undertook to set up stronger administrative officers politically accountable to elected councils, made much less headway in New England than in other areas of the country.[16]

The town meeting tradition was based on the Puritan principle that all members of the town congregation should be educated to read Scripture and understand its teaching and, in political affairs, to understand public policies and control their elected officers. It worked reasonably well on the small scale of the rural town. With a relatively homogeneous electorate, a highly literate citizenry, and sophisticated leadership, the early New England society almost justified Walter Bagehot's observation that such a society, if separated from the rest of America, could make a parliamentary cabinet system work admirably.[17]

In the nineteenth century, however, direct democracy proved to have less internal discipline. In ecclesiastical matters, the idea that all believers should be able to read and interpret Scripture for themselves led in many sects to the idea that they did not need much help from a specially educated clergy. The most rapidly growing churches were not those like the Unitarian, Episcopalian, and Presbyterian with high educational qualifications for the ministry but those that took literally the priesthood of all believers, regardless of their training.

In the South and parts of the Midwest, the more populist segments of the Baptist churches and various evangelistic sects of even less rigorous educational standards set the political tone in the nineteenth century. It was this approach—by no means confined to those regions—that led to the long ballot, in which great numbers of minor administrative officers were elected by popular vote, and to the consequent breakdown of executive discipline and exaggeration of the role of lawyers and the courts in administrative affairs. These habits still had their influence in the twentieth century in local government as Georgia and Tennessee were as resistant as Massachusetts and Connecticut to the city-manager form of local government.[18]

Many evangelists professed the hope that if all believers could be induced to read and interpret the Scriptures for themselves, the faithful would be led to reject the self-interested claims of other denominations and accept the obvious evidence of Scripture in favor of their own correct theology.

One of the most idealistic and peculiarly American among them was Alexander Campbell, who wanted the movement he founded to avoid any "denomination"—any particular designation other than that of the Church of Christ—and to profess no creed other than the Bible itself. In their political significance, his ideas were peculiarly American in several ways. His reliance on the ability of every believer to interpret Scripture for himself was the basis for his distrust of political as well as ecclesiastical hierarchy, for his emphasis on a legalistic way of thinking, and for his sympathy with the rational science of his era. His theology, which was in rebellion against the Scottish Calvinism of his ancestors, was closely allied with that of the ultrafundamentalist Sandemanian movement in Britain of which Michael Faraday was a devoted adherent. (Faraday, the discoverer of electromagnetic induction, as a dissenter could not have any status in Oxford or Cambridge, and had to depend on the Royal Institution for his support.)[19]

Campbell was sympathetic to science: the first college that his churches founded, at Georgetown, Kentucky, in 1836, was Bacon College, named in honor of Francis Bacon to register approval of his empirical philosophy. It was moved to Harrodsburg, Kentucky, then discontinued in 1850, but in 1865 reestablished in Lexington where it acquired the property, and fragments of the original tradition, of Transylvania University.

Campbell was also sympathetic to causes that were liberal in the context of the early nineteenth century. He disapproved, for example, of secular laws to require observance of Sunday.[20] And he favored extension of the franchise: in the Virginia state Constitutional Convention of 1829 he led the unsuccessful campaign for the removal of the property qualification for voting, in hopes that such a reform would benefit the antislavery movement, against James Madison and others who were more conservative in their constitutional theories. The movement that Campbell helped found, however, soon split into various segments, each vowing that it would not become a separate denomination but represent the general body of Christianity as a whole. But they divided nonetheless, some with advanced and others with reactionary ecclesiastical ideas. Direct democracy again failed to produce agreement.[21]

The early American scientists, beginning with the Puritans and amalgamating with the Jeffersonian tradition, were persuaded that science would be a liberating political force, weakening traditional authority and strengthening democracy. Modern scientists recognize both that science now has a profound impact on public affairs and that it is difficult for the lay public to understand. But many of them have inherited the old dissenting view that no effort should be spared to have everyone read and understand the sources from which truth is derived. Scientific societies, philanthropic foundations, government agencies, and television networks all seek in one way or another to increase the public understanding of science.

The goal is ideal, and the efforts have surely had some significant success. But it would be easy to rely too much on that process. The temptation to have issues decided by public referenda and to have politicians controlled by the samplers of public opinion can be carried so far as to weaken the competence and the responsibility of those in elected office. The vision that a scientifically literate public should some day be able to decide each major issue instantly by an electronic referendum is likely to run up against the political difficulties that plagued the early religious dissenters. The truth has to be interpreted in its application, and those who interpret it—or who frame the question for the referendum—will be involved in the competition for status and power.

While in some ways religion and science are similar in their impact on government, they differ widely in the United States in one conspicuous way: the government does not give financial support directly for a religious establishment, but it gives big money to create a scientific establishment, while leaving it surprisingly free to dissent. The American university scientist can serve on some of the hundreds of advisory committees to high political authority while retaining his independent base and tenure at a university. He has free access to congressional committees, which court independent scientists as a counterbalance to the in-house scientists. And he can take part with great independence in the many committees of the National Academy of Sciences and its affiliates or the dozens of think tanks supported either by government or by special interest groups seeking to influence government policy. As Congress continues to seek independent scientific advice, apart from or in competition with the executive departments, these roles become increasingly influential.

It is of course difficult to define the scientific community or to think about it as if it had any political point of view or attitude in common. The National Academy of Sciences with its National Research Council is clearly the elite organization among research societies, and the major one formally chartered by Act of Congress. It is usually led by men who have had extensive experience in work on public policy as well as on basic research. Consequently it tends to behave in policy issues rather like an established church, formally independent of government, even though mainly supported by it, and always under criticism from the dissenting sectarians.

Among the dissenters there is a widespread spectrum of political sentiment ranging from critical independence of judgment to political activism of a radical nature. The Federation of American Scientists, for example, is the heir to the group of atomic scientists who immediately after the Second World War began to be critical of the slowness of the United States to organize international action for the control of atomic energy and particularly nuclear weapons. The Council for a Livable World and the Union of Concerned Scientists have had somewhat similar purposes. These efforts by scientists have been supported by many religious organizations which appreciate the threat of nuclear warfare and join in demands for legislative action or public referenda to stop the use of nuclear power or put a freeze on the development of nuclear weapons. The Society for Social Responsibility in Science and the Scientists and Engineers for Social and Political Action are among the other continuing political groups that are highly critical of what they consider to be the political orthodoxy of the National Academy.[22]

Quite aside from the lobbies of the scientists themselves, there are many organizations of laymen, including consulting firms and associations of volunteers, which undertake to act politically on the basis of more or less scientific concerns about public issues. They range from valid and sensible programs, like many in the environmental protection campaign, to movements based on new kinds of superstition decked out in scientific terminology—such as the Church of Scientology or the organizations that attack the teaching of evolution.

Political action by the scientists' organizations is often directed to either the legislative or the judicial process, especially when the organizations are on the liberal or radical side of issues. The influence of psychologists on the courts to eliminate segregation in the public schools, the pressure of the atomic scientists for stricter safety standards for nuclear power plants, and the campaigns for regulation of experiments in genetic engineering are all examples. But legislative action is also the strategy when the purpose is to protect the independence of science from politics.

When scientists decided to ask for government money on a large scale in 1945, they were afraid to do so on any basis that would invite centralized political control. Neither the leading scientists nor members of the Congress were prepared to support a system by which government, by its control of the necessary funds, would make the basic decisions on research strategy.

To prevent the creation of any centralized science establishment, the first step was to have the government give out research funds through a variety of departments and agencies and not through a single organization. Each of the three military departments and several civilian agencies came to compete with the National Science Foundation for the work of private scientific institutions, with the line between their applied interests and the basic research for the foundation being inevitably blurred in practice.

The second step was to avoid having funds allocated by congressional appropriation acts to individual universities or to particular states (as had been the earlier practice with respect to agricultural research funds). By maintaining the principle that the basic division of the funds was to be by scientific discipline and then within each discipline by specific projects, it would be clear that politicians lacked the expertise to make decisions, which would have to be entrusted to committees of scientists.

The project grant system then made it possible for the big dispensers of grant funds (such as the National Institutes of Health or the Department of Defense) to play a mediating role between those dedicated to a faith in pure science and those concerned with the resulting applications. The dispensing agency must not only convince the researcher that he is free to pursue basic research without distortion for applied purposes but also convince members of Congress that the results of the research are predestined to work out for the prosperity of mankind as well as the greater glory of science. While this approach has made basic science relatively prosperous by earlier standards, it has involved a certain amount of hypocrisy on the part of scientists and skepticism on the part of philanthropists and politicians. There are even a few scientists in America who envy the approach of their British colleagues, who get more of their government funds through the universities from a unified establishment, the University Grants Committee, which needs to make less pretense of practical application in its relations with the government. The British university scientists are not expected to justify their support by undertaking projects that promise practical benefits; their status is like that of the clergy in the old establishment. The Parliament is of course interested in ultimate applications. But it is trained not to interfere in an establishment's detailed affairs. It does not make specific allocations either to particular universities or to projects, and in return the pure academic tradition discourages the scientist from taking part in political issues, much as the old monastic orders encouraged meditation on the true faith in isolation from the world of affairs.

Religious issues that are purely doctrinal can be left undecided in the present world since we are willing to tolerate a plurality of sects. Purely scientific issues can also be left undecided, left for ultimate settlement by experiment and debate among academics. But it has become obvious that, as a result of the achievements of scientists, the relation between abstract thought and practical consequences is now so close that an arrangement like that of the old ideal of the separation of church and state—*i.e.,* a separation of religious and scientific institutions from political action—is more difficult to maintain. Unfortunately for this ideal, the concerns of religion and science are now intermingled. Nuclear disarmament, genetic engineering, euthanasia, abortion, environmental pollution, the teaching of evolution in public schools—all now involve organized action by scientific as well as religious groups. Each effort typically involves the lobbying of congressional committees, supported by appeals to the voters, in order to decide some specific issue by specific legislation.

The approach of direct democracy thus usually takes the form of expanding the rule of law, and the approach is frequently influential and effective as long as the subject matter can usefully be set apart from other subjects and decided in isolation. Such a sectarian approach in science, however, is not always useful. The National Academy of Sciences, hoping to be able to exert independent influence on major issues by the provision of scientific advice, set up a Committee on Science and Public Policy in 1962. Its work and the reports of various committees from specific disciplines were effective on many specific problems, but on the one topic scientists thought about most often—the question how to distribute federal financial support among the various competing scientific disciplines—the committee could not agree on how to advise the Congress.

The question, unfortunately, is typical of the most significant shortcoming of science in its contribution to public policy. Some of the most difficult and significant issues arise at the points where one program competes or conflicts with another. High drama is usually a matter, not of a simple conflict between good and evil, but of a conflict among competing goods. How science struggles with such conflict within the governmental system is our next question.

Compromise and Coordination

In order to make coherent and consistent decisions on such issues, a government needs the support of a more disciplined system than the United States has managed to develop. Such discipline is not supplied by occasional forceful and brilliant presidential leadership on a few major current issues; it requires the pervasive control by the heads of departments and bureaus of the hundreds of secondary issues on which the major ones depend and the kind of long-range planning that can set policy priorities and that can be done only by a strong career staff. On such issues, party discipline may be helpful, but it must depend on the willingness of those in public life to support decisions on issues in which fundamental values are in conflict.

Such willingness is partly a matter of basic attitudes, but partly too it depends on the existence of career incentives for those who must do the staff work on which political action must depend. As we think about public career systems, we usually concentrate on the government. But among the nonprofit institutions in American society—those professing to represent the public interest rather than competitive market forces—the government service competes with religious and scientific and educational institutions for personnel and influence. The extension of governmental powers and expenditures does not always strengthen the government career services in this competition. One may get a hint of this by looking at the growth of federal expenditures since shortly after the Second World War and comparing it with the expansion of the federal civil service, which has not increased in proportion to the growth of population. On the other hand, federal tax deductions and the expansion of federal grants and contracts have vastly increased the career opportunities in research institutions, professional associations of state and local officials, universities, and philanthropic foundations. None of these pays financial dividends, but each is deeply committed to some particular concept of the public interest. All of them, together with the civil service, constitute a kind of establishment but, paradoxically, an establishment of dissenters, many of whom are antigovernment in their convictions.

It would be hard to count the corporate entities which get federal funds to carry on activities that are essentially public in nature. They range from military policy studies by munitions-makers to the activities of impeccably conservative professional institutions to the programs of welfare groups and civil rights activists. This practice aroused the indignation of the national director of the Conservative Caucus, Howard Phillips, who listed 175 "left-leaning groups that get your tax dollars" and proposed to cut off their federal funds. His list ranged over a wide political spectrum; the AFL-CIO and the American Bar Association were listed, along with the Martin L. King, Jr., Center for Social Change, the Environmental Defense Fund, and the National Council of Churches. "Billions of taxpayer dollars," he argued, "are being dispatched annually to organizations which seek to influence our cultural, economic, political, and religious life," and this practice is an offense against the principle of the First Amendment to the Constitution forbidding federal support of a religious establishment.[23]

This diversity of federal support for political activities has great disadvantages in terms of public accountability. It fails to supply a disciplined staff at the center of public policy, committed to a common approach based on some similarity of educational background. During its first half century, it did not seem impossible that the United States might develop such a service; the Jacksonian period brought almost as many college-educated men into top appointments as had the Federalists. But fewer of them came from the Puritan colleges of the northeast, and more from the middle states and the South.[24] And the common efforts of Jefferson and Adams to create a national university were defeated by the jealousy of the rival private colleges, eager to protect their religious interests against a potentially godless competitor supported by taxation. By the time the civil service system was finally established, the land-grant colleges had been created and were about to supply the specialists in the competing agricultural and mechanic arts to staff the specialized bureaus of the government.

The history of the British Administrative Class is, of course, very different. That career system derived directly from the habits of the established church, of which the sovereign was the head. The educational system on which those careers were based was, in the nineteenth century, the same for ecclesiastical and administrative careers: education at Oxford and Cambridge in the classics and other humanities, without much special attention to the specific problems to be faced in the later career. The Anglican clergy in the nineteenth century, for example, were poorly educated in theology by comparison with their Scottish Presbyterian or Roman Catholic counterparts. A gentlemanly education was considered sufficient for either public vocation.[25]

Such a system was tolerant of divergent opinions, as long as they were maintained discreetly and did not challenge public authority. From this point of view, even in the United States some intellectual leaders found the Anglican establishment attractive. It could afford to compromise in order to be comprehensive; it could tolerate—especially among the laity—a wide divergence of theological beliefs, or hardly any at all, in order to serve its purpose as the official state religion.

Without the tolerant ethical attitudes of an establishment, and the career incentives and educational system on which it is based, the United States now finds that its approach to policy decisions in its administrative career services is complicated by the strong views of specialists in religious groups and in scientific institutions. They are mutually uncomprehending and antagonistic, and yet they behave in similar ways in relation to political action. And in both cases, their actions are the result not altogether of their own philosophy but of the temptations that arise from their interaction with political factions.

If evangelical religious leaders had followed the doctrines of their earlier and more intellectual leaders (which they have rarely done), they might have been more tolerant with regard to personal behavior and more concerned with those basic issues of faith that cannot be dealt with by public policy. But for purposes of political action the so-called fundamentalists have been less concerned with the fundamentals of doctrine than with political action. The scientist, in a similar fashion, is rarely concerned dispassionately with processes of cause and effect; the temptation is too great to be an active cause of the application of knowledge to the right ends.

Quite aside from the influence that religious and scientific leaders exercise on their own initiative, both are involved in political issues in which political leaders share the initiative, with results that are laudable or regrettable, depending on one's point of view. The campaigns for the abolition of slavery and the adoption of the prohibition amendment involved religious leaders as well as ambitious politicians. In these and similar issues, the popular evangelical leadership had to contend with the lukewarm or compromising attitudes of some of the more enlightened and intellectual churches.

After the New Deal, and especially after the Second World War, on those issues in which the nation saw a conflict between rigorous principle and political compromise, it was the scientists who played the key intellectual roles. From the point of view of the politician or administrator, the scientific specialist behaved much like his dissenting predecessor.

This was less of a problem in the United Kingdom, where the established civil service played a role in supporting gentlemanly compromise analogous to that of the established church a century or two earlier. The British scientist in the career civil service has none of the direct public access to political authority that his American counterpart enjoys. The ethos of the civil service generalist supports quiet subordination to the final judgments of politicians and commonsense compromise in policy recommendations. This ethos has to be based on the practice of excluding cantankerous scientific specialists from official deliberations. But in the United States, the intellectual qualities of the scientist give politicians a chance to defend rigid policy views and oppose compromise, for two reasons.

First of all, the typical scientist is trained to seek precision in what he learns by the use of methods that colleagues can replicate and confirm. The incentives of his calling encourage him to concentrate on those aspects of a problem that are material and quantifiable and to pay less attention to those that involve imponderable value judgments. He therefore finds it awkward to compromise not only with specialists from other disciplines than his own but with generalists who seek to moderate or dilute his precise recommendations with commonsense judgment or political expediency. By contrast with the typical scientist, the experienced leaders of the scientific elite are troubled by the approach of their less sophisticated colleagues to policy issues, in much the same way that the more sophisticated theologians are embarrassed by the simple formulas of the Moral Majority.

Second, the approach of the scientist to public issues today may be complicated by feelings of guilt that are nearly as profound as those that tortured John Bunyan. For more than three centuries, roughly since Francis Bacon, scientists lived in the happy conviction that they were part of a movement that was steadily increasing freedom, as well as making people in general more healthy, wealthy, and wise. But all that has changed. The atomic bomb came first; Oppenheimer's classic statement that scientists had now known sin was a starter. That might have been forgotten but for the growing sense in many fields that technology was no longer a guarantee of perpetual progress but a possible threat to human survival, and sensitive scientists felt guilty about the public misuse of their pure knowledge. Genetic or psychological manipulation as the basis of a new tyranny, environmental degradation and the overcrowding of population, and nuclear warfare—such visions of a new hell have made many scientists unwilling to think of their relation to public issues except in terms of uncompromising defense of their personal convictions. The political action organizations which they have founded give them full scope for public dissent from the establishment's compromises.

The use of science to prevent reasonable compromise cannot be blamed mainly on the scientists. Much as the uncompromising attitude on social issues like prohibition was the work less of sophisticated theologians than of politicians who made use of their preaching, so the use of scientific findings in support of rigid policy stands is often the work of political and not scientific leaders. The tremendous field of environmental and health regulation offers the best example. Scientists, by making it possible to identify and measure environmental pollutants or carcinogenic drugs in quantities so minuscule (in some cases, parts per trillion) that they could not have been detected a generation ago, have set the stage for the debate between politicians who see the possibility of more effective protection of the health of the public and those who wish to avoid ridiculous and unnecessary constraints on economic productivity.

In the government's regulation of food safety, for example, it has been scientists who argued for recognizing that the scientific determination of a particular risk—notably, the minute risk of cancer from the use of saccharin—was not an adequate basis for the prohibition of a substance, since such risks could be proved for many essential foods. It was scientists who argued that risks had to be balanced against economic and other benefits in ways that could not be calculated scientifically and so required administrative judgment and discretion. That was the majority judgment of the scientists who took part in a study for Congress by the Institute of Medicine. Congress, however, preferred in principle not to permit any such administrative discretion and accepted instead the minority views of the scientists on the study, leaving in effect the earlier law based on the "zero-tolerance" theory absolutely prohibiting the sale of any food additive with the most minute carcinogenic danger. But then, with an inconsistency recalling the Prohibition-era politicians who voted dry but drank wet, the Congress enacted a law forbidding the Food and Drug Administration to enforce the ban on saccharin which its earlier statute had required.[26]

The same political tendency appears in fields in which the social sciences are conspicuous. The tendency of the scientists themselves to emphasize the aspects of a policy to which their particular disciplines are relevant leads them to highly specialized, if not distorted, views on an issue. The testimony of an economist on tax or fiscal policy is one example, and that of a sociologist on urban housing or affirmative action is another; such scientists all too rarely realize that they are talking about different aspects of the same problem. Even when the economist takes into account the sociological aspects of his problem, or vice versa, neither is likely to give enough weight to the nonscientific aspects, namely those aspects concerned with justice and political power. The politician, however, will be eager to find one or another type of scientific testimony to buttress his prejudices and thus be reenforced in his disposition not to unite with a responsible political party in support of a total program and, above all, not to delegate adequate discretion to general administrators to help formulate new approaches to difficult problems.

The tendency of the scientist to emphasize an abstract and specialized view of the truth now complicates the problem of developing a political system that can make responsible decisions on complex issues. In this, it is reminiscent of the emphasis of the early Puritans on faith, especially on faith in a particular dissenting dogma. The two tendencies have in turn made it hard to develop a political system that can achieve a proper balance between fundamental science and its practical applications or between administrative authority and either populist politics or rigid legalism. But these are petty inconveniences by comparison with the disastrous effects of moving too far in the opposite direction—the direction of either an orthodox religious establishment or a scientific ideology. To that danger we may now well devote brief attention.

III

Social Perfectibility and Human Engineering

Thomas Jefferson remarked that enlightened skeptics in Protestant countries became Deists, but in Catholic countries, atheists.[1] That generalization may have been entirely too sweeping to be reliable, but it suggests another tempting and equally risky one. The revolutions that began with the rise of science in the seventeenth century led Britain and America, predominantly Protestant countries, to have high hopes for science as the instrument of human progress but never tempted them to make scientific institutions into a new established church. But in the countries where there had never been an effective ecclesiastical Reformation, revolutionary movements tried to make science into a new political faith, a new doctrinal basis for an intolerant secular establishment. As a result, while the political institutions of the United States and Great Britain evolved along divergent lines during the nineteenth century, that divergence was much less wide than the split that separated the two of them from the radical movements of continental Europe.

The difference began to be apparent as American sympathizers with the French encyclopedists and *philosophes* were shocked by the French revolution, not only by the cruelties of the Jacobin terror but perhaps even more by Robespierre's efforts to convert Jean Jacques Rousseau's Deism into a new state religion. From that time on, while Americans differed from the British in decentralizing their administrative institutions and legislative leadership, they were far more strongly opposed to the political ideology of the main revolutionary movements on the Continent.

Do we account for these differences by attributing their origins to philosophical or theological ideas? Or do we attribute them to economic or technological developments or to basic geographic factors? Was the growth of freedom made possible in Great Britain and the United States by their geographic isolation from the threat of invasion by European powers and then glorified after the fact by patriotic scholars? Was Puritan dissenting doctrine responsible for the interest in science and the growth of commercial activity, or was that doctrine more the search of a new economic class for an ethos more congenial to its interests than the old orthodox theology?

It seems reasonable to conclude that there is always an interaction of theoretical ideas and practical social or economic movements. Robert K. Merton, whose work on the early relationship of Puritanism to science has been so influential, remarks that the interaction between the influence of ideas and that of class or economic interests is a two-way process that cannot be measured precisely.[2] It seems (at least to me) equally reasonable to conclude that the process is not two-way—merely between theory and sociological or economic interests—but three-way, also involving practical institutional habits and traditional constitutional patterns of action.

The struggles in Western Europe during the nineteenth century pitted new ideas against old institutions. There the revolutionary movements were limited in their success by the opposition of entrenched establishments, and they varied greatly in the intensity and the duration of their devotion to their initial ideologies. The French, whose intellectual ferment started the upheavals in Europe, oscillated throughout the nineteenth century between spasms of radical insurrection and the restoration of dynastic rule—or later, the installation of equally stodgy bourgeois republicanism. The German and Central European states had their periods of upheaval but, throughout most of the century, maintained their traditional monarchies in uneasy power. But in all of them, under revolutionary and reactionary regimes alike, the central administrative systems, with their permanent bureaucracies and standing armies, stubbornly held on to the main levers of power.

The main intellectual foundation of these bureaucracies, as they continued after a fashion to serve their political masters of varying traditions—royal, republican, and revolutionary alike—was the heritage of the Roman civil law as developed by the medieval clergy and as modernized under Frederick the Great and Napoleon. It set the government apart from and over the general run of the population; its concern for the maintenance of power and official privilege was paramount over its belief in the faith or the ideology to which it paid polite deference. As stubborn as these institutional systems were, however, they were shaken by the main currents of thought that periodically revolutionized Europe and that in our time left it divided between the Communist world and its uneasy rivals in the West.

Where the old bureaucracies were successfully challenged, it was by political ideologies that were based on faith in science. Science had been associated loosely with the earlier revolutions in England and America, but there, it was more an ally than an enemy of religious faith. Although the continental Enlightenment tolerated some such intellectual compromise in its early phases, the French *philosophes* moved rather more generally toward a thoroughgoing materialist position, somewhat to the discomfort of a Deist like Voltaire.[3] By the Victorian era, the skepticism of a Hume or a Gibbon had become less fashionable in Britain, while in France and on the Continent the antireligious rationalists became more inclined to assert a faith in scientific materialism as a political dogma.

The most conspicuous leader among them in the early nineteenth century was Auguste Comte (1798–1857), the self-proclaimed inventor of sociology, advocate of positivism, and founder of the Religion of Humanity. As a political theorist he ranks in contemporary opinion well below some other nineteenth-century philosophers, but he is worth recalling here because of the strong opinion he expressed about science and its influence on politics—a line of thought that later was developed both by Marx for the Communists and by Herbert Spencer for the believers in laissez-faire economics.

Comte's central theory was that humanity had passed through the ages of theology and of metaphysics and was now ready for the stage of positivism: science was gradually extending its domain along a spectrum from the more rigorous and quantitative sciences, such as astronomy and physics, through chemistry and biology, and would soon create a science of society, in which basic values and political decisions ought to be subject to positive scientific determination.[4] By a process of social evolution such a scientific approach would, he believed, surely lead mankind along a path of inevitable progress to moral as well as material improvement and to a state approaching a perfect society. His belief in progress set him firmly against the old political forces of order, which in Europe were supported by the Catholic hierarchy. But as much as he disapproved of the conservative and Catholic forces of contemporary European politics, he was even more contemptuous of nineteenth-century liberalism. What he wanted was far more like the institutions of the old oppressive ecclesiastical establishment than like the easy-going tolerant system of the Enlightenment.

In his theoretical ideas, he was bitterly critical of Voltaire and Rousseau, whom he called "incomplete destructives," and he affirmed that his own intellectual roots went back through politically conservative theorists like David Hume and Joseph de Maistre to Thomas Aquinas.[5] He proclaimed that "we Sociocrats are no more democrats than aristocrats."

As for his institutional approach, he proposed to fight the old order, not by ordinary secular politics, but by creating a new church. This was not to be based on Rousseau's pallid Deism, nor Robespierre's worship of a supreme being, but on a new Positive Religion, the worship of "the true Great Being," namely Humanity. But *Humanity* was defined "as *the whole* of human beings, past, present and future. The word *whole* points out clearly that you must not take in all men, but those only who are really assimilable, in virtue of a real co-operation towards the common existence. . . . mere digesting machines are no real part of Humanity."[6]

In his later years, Comte summed up this religious and political system that had been elaborated in a series of massive scholarly volumes in his *Catechism of Positive Religion*, which was intended for general readers and especially for women. His new system was to depend on "two powers, the spiritual and the temporal." The spiritual power, clearly to be superior, was put in the new priesthood, "the soul of the true sociocracy," whose members were to be selected by the supreme head of the order. The temporal power was to be in the "patriciate," with a far greater concentration of control over the industrial system than the capitalist system had provided and with full right of inheritance. Under this system, "the priesthood will make the proletaries deeply conscious of the real advantages of their social condition. . . . The happiness springing from a noble submission and from a just freedom from responsibility will be unceasingly appreciated by them."[7]

Comte, shortly after Louis Napoleon had come to power as president of France, wrote that his own "resolution was greatly strengthened by the fortunate crisis which has just abolished the parliamentary regime and instituted a dictatorial republic." He disapproved not only of parliamentary regimes but of any governments that were controlled by popular elections. He acknowledged that his proposed system called for a "severe regime . . . too antipathetic to our present mental state for it ever to prevail without the irresistible support of women and the proletaries." And it was especially women on whom he relied; it was solely among women, he wrote, "that, at the present day, we can find the noble submissiveness of spirit required for a systematic regeneration. During the last four years, the reason of the people has suffered profoundly from the unfortunate exercise of universal suffrage. . . . I see none anywhere but women, who, as a consequence of their wholesome exclusion from political action, can give me the support required." To strengthen the appropriate feminist attitude, he declared that marriage was better without sex, proposed that widowhood be permanent, and suggested that every woman "must be carefully secured from work away from home."[8] His position on such issues may be attributed to his own personal misfortunes and psychological problems; he depended for some years for financial support on his wife's earnings as a prostitute, had his scholarly work interrupted for two years by mental illness, and had a platonic love affair much later with a woman whose death left him in a state of mystical despair.

It is clearly unfair to Comte to put so much emphasis on his later mystical phase, which may obscure his contribution as a scientific sociologist. But this personal transition is in some ways paralleled

by the conversion of science into a political mystique as revolutionaries made it the basis for their political faith. The intellectual leader
of these revolutions was of course Karl Marx. How much he owed
any of his ideas to Comte is hard to estimate, but clearly his materialist dialectic is similar to Comte's positivism, and his elite party
to Comte's priesthood. His preeminent position as the theoretician
of communism does not need to be restated here.

For the purposes of this essay, it may be more significant to note
the way in which natural scientists and philosophers of science in
the late nineteenth century contributed to the leadership of revolutionary political thought. While science was mixed up with various
eccentric fads like mesmerism, phrenology, and spiritualism, it was
also involved with the more serious types of Utopian radicalism in
Central and Eastern Europe. (England was an exception; Thomas
Henry Huxley, for example, affirmed that he was "utterly opposed"
to "the creation of an Established Church Scientific, with a hierarchical organization and a professorial Episcopate."[9] On the other
hand, the most advanced science in the German states as well as in
France supplied many of the leaders of revolutionary political thought.
Rudolf Virchow, a leading anthropologist and founder of cellular pa-
thology, as a medical scientist tried to establish a thoroughgoing
mechanistic conception of life, and as a politician led the liberal
opposition to Bismarck in the Reichstag.[10]

Obviously the natural sciences in this way of thinking had to provide a new approach, replacing philosophy, idealistic ethics, and
metaphysics as the ultimate guide to thought and action. The arguments to this effect by Ludwig Feuerbach, the German philosopher (1804–1872) helped to provide the transition from Hegelian
idealism to Marxist revolutionary doctrine. Nicholas Chernyshevsky (1828–1889), the son of an Orthodox priest and a leader in the
development of bolshevism, picked up the new ideas and helped set
Lenin on the road to making Marxism the new revolutionary faith.
As Adam Ulam observes, "Chernyshevsky (and he was not alone)
having rejected Christianity never lost the need for faith, for absolute certainty."[11] This faith no longer dealt with religious beliefs but
with scientific ideology.

But how could an ardent revolutionary reconcile belief in scientific determinism, a mechanistic materialism that explained everything in terms of rigorous causes and effects, with an appeal for self-sacrificing political action? The question was by no means overlooked. Revolutionary theorists were quite capable of reconciling their faith in the inevitability of the triumph of the proletariat with their appeals to the workers for dedicated and disciplined participation in the class struggle and in a revolution to make the inevitable come true.

In this respect, of course, the "scientific" revolutionaries were not entirely different from the earlier radicals whose dedication rested on religious faith. The sense of being in harmony with an irresistible movement toward ultimate triumph does not dull the taste for energetic action. The doctrine of scientific determinism was no more difficult to reconcile with free political will than had been the old Calvinist theory of predestination. The Westminster Confession of Faith, which the Long Parliament approved in 1647, proclaimed God's complete foreknowledge of all that would ever come to pass and the total inability of all men to do good works except by the grace of God. But it then went on to say that the elect "ought to be diligent in stirring up the grace of God that is in them."[12] This doctrine produced radical political action in the seventeenth century but could be circulated in Presbyterian Sunday schools in the twentieth century without noticeable upheavals.

However difficult it may seem to reconcile a belief in either divine predestination or scientific inevitability with a commitment to self-sacrificing and dedicated action, it is clear that the Puritan reformers and the Marxist revolutionaries both managed to do so. It is also clear that, as the original flush of zeal wore off, their dedication came to be diluted by self-interest, material success, and a desire for political power. Between the two movements, however, there was one all-important difference. The Puritans and their Deist successors, unlike the Marxists of Eastern Europe, did not wind up supporting tyranny.

This is not to say that the Puritans did not begin by trying. From Calvin's Geneva to early Massachusetts, there were many efforts to use political power to enforce religious conformity. But the fact that these efforts were made and failed suggests that, while the temptation to power may corrupt any system of politics, whether or not that corruption will be absolute and nearly irreversible may depend on how people think about the ends of politics.

One clue may lie in the question of human perfectibility—the question whether the ideal political system or the ideal religious discipline can bring about a state of social perfection. It was the vision of freeing society from the conflicts of political parties and elections, and perfecting it by the certainties of science, that captured the imagination of Comte and his more effective revolutionary successors. The faith in perfectibility has led not only to eccentric and isolated Utopian experiments—such as the Fourierist phalansteries and the communal farms of upper New England and northern New York State[13]—but also to the sustained large-scale despotism of a single-party state. In the contemporary world, of course, such despotic systems have been created by the Marxist revolutions, professing their foundations in a comprehensive ideology of science.

As Leszek Kolakowski put it after renouncing his early Communist philosophy and defecting from Communist Poland, the idea "that we can design some plan for the whole of society whereby harmony, justice, and plenty are attained by human engineering is an invitation for despotism." The aspiration to social perfection by means of human engineering and the belief that the ends justify the means lead clearly to tyranny. "Any social Utopia which purports to offer a technical blueprint for the perfect society now strikes me as pregnant with the most terrible dangers."[14]

If leading scholars are not sure whether the difference between free and tyrannical—or between radical and reactionary—regimes is one of political beliefs or merely of historical and economic circumstances, practical politicians are equally confused. In the United States we are still quarreling over how we should think about those foreign governments that restrict civil rights. Does it matter whether they do so out of devotion to radical ideology or only because their history and social background keep them from behaving in a more civilized manner?[15]

The issue comes up especially with respect to some of the Latin American republics. The history of those republics shows how complex an interaction there is between philosophical and pragmatic influences in the evolution of free institutions. As in the United States, revolutionaries in Latin America were shielded by the barrier of the Atlantic Ocean against easy military domination from Europe, and the skepticism of the Enlightenment had weakened the influence of the ecclesiastical establishment that had always been the strong supporter of the colonial monarchies. The Latin American revolutions were distinguished from that of the United States, however, both in the way they looked backward and in their forward vision. Their political institutions had been shaped by the Spanish army and the hierarchy of the Catholic church, both of which sought to create a centralized system of government in order to spread the only true faith. And the new institutions after the revolution suffered by following a Utopian vision: as Simón Bolívar himself, the great liberator of South America, put it in 1812, "The codes consulted by our lawmakers were . . . the inventions of well-meaning visionaries, who, thinking in terms of ideal republics, sought to attain political perfection on the supposition of the perfectability of the human race."[16]

It is ironic that in several countries of Latin America today it is the Catholic hierarchy that is the strongest influence for the protection of popular rights against the oppression of the civil and military authorities. That is enough to warn us against making too doctrinaire an issue of the influence of ideas, whether theological or scientific, over political institutions. A fifteenth-century church that was deeply committed to freeing Spain from Moorish rule and a military that was tempted by the gold and silver of the Aztecs and Incas had pragmatic incentives, not dependent on theological doctrines, to build up the authoritarian power of the dynasty in Madrid.

Yet the importance of the way people thought and believed should not be discounted. The belief in the total depravity of man, the foundation of Puritan theology, worked against the maintenance of any ecclesiastical establishment and its support of authoritarian government. Belief in the perfectibility of mankind, on the contrary, was and is a great temptation to the institution of an all-powerful authority, dominated by a small elite.

Between these two extreme beliefs, the Roman Catholic doctrine, holding that the church is identified with the Kingdom of God and is the sole dispenser of grace may seem closer to the perfectionist extreme. But it is not quite at that extreme since it holds too with the doctrine of Saint Augustine, whose views on the total depravity of mankind were the forerunner of later Calvinist thought. On the other hand, there remained in Christian theology traces of the gnostic ideas derived from Greek philosophy, which encouraged the belief that baptism cured the believer of sin. Reinhold Niebuhr notes that this tendency to believe that man may actually be made perfect by accepting the doctrine and the discipline of the church was especially prevalent in the Eastern Orthodox church. He quotes a recent Orthodox theologian, Chrestos Androustos: "The remission of sin is not the mere imputation of freedom from sin,—but the actual effacement of it. . . . The state of sin is removed entirely by God's power in the act of justification." To the extent that the sacraments of the church were thought to make mankind actually righteous, the faithful in Russia and the eastern Mediterranean countries were tempted to support an elite ecclesiastical establishment.[17]

One need not believe that such doctrinal differences are completely responsible for the way in which political institutions have evolved in order to be impressed by certain parallels in historical development. It is the countries where the Calvinist doctrine of original sin and total depravity weakened the authority of any ecclesiastical establishment that refused in their political revolutions to let science become the basis of a radical ideology.

At the other extreme, it was Russia, the political base of the Orthodox church after the Turks took Constantinople, that carried forward the doctrine of human perfectibility. When it rejected that doctrine in theological terms, it committed itself to work for perfection under a new priesthood—the Communist party—under the guidance of a scientific ideology. If in Russia the real working scientists look on the new priesthood of the Party with cynical scorn, their reaction is not very different from the attitude of religious idealists toward the old clergy.

If one were determined to prove the influence of abstract ideas on practical political developments, it would be tempting to stop at this point. But while it may seem highly probable that the idea of perfectibility contributes to autocratic politics, it is even more clear that it does not always lead in that direction.

Let us take as an illustration the scholar whose influence over the development of sociology in Britain and the United States was even greater than Comte's, Herbert Spencer (1820–1903). Spencer, who came from a dissenting family with ties to the intellectual tradition of Joseph Priestley, was similar to Comte in many of his views—in his skepticism about organized religion (although he bore out Jefferson's dictum by being more of a Deist than an atheist), his belief in social evolution, and his confidence in the influence of science on human progress, which was perhaps confirmed by his early working experience as an engineer.

On the issue of the perfectibility of mankind, Spencer was more forthright than Comte, who occasionally shied away from what he called "the fanciful extravagance of unlimited perfectibility."[18] Spencer had fewer qualms, at least in theory. In his *Social Statics* he outlined his faith in progress by an evolutionary process which amounted to a "universal law; and . . . in virtue of that law it must continue until the state we call perfection is reached." Progress, he argued, "is not an accident, but a necessity. . . . so surely must the human faculties be moulded into complete fitness for the social state; so surely must the things we call evil and immorality disappear; so surely must man become perfect." Spencer was confident in progress toward perfection because he believed that "God wills man's happiness," which must be attained by his "liberty to do all that his faculties naturally impel him to do. Then God intends he should have that liberty."[19]

With this emphasis on liberty, Spencer, for all his theoretical confidence in the ultimate perfectibility of man, was skeptical—especially in his later works—about deliberate and organized efforts toward that end, especially by government: "human nature," he wrote, "though indefinitely modifiable, can be modified but very slowly. . . . all laws and institutions and appliances which count on getting from it, within a short time, much better results than present ones, will inevitably fail."[20] On this issue, he challenged Comte directly. Comte, he wrote, although avowedly for an industrial state, was so French in his way of thinking that he "prescribes arrangements characteristic of a militant type" rather than those appropriate for free industrial enterprise; under the "militant type," he said, government dominates the economy and "the individual is owned by the State."[21]

Spencer had rather more influence in the United States than in Great Britain. In both countries the ideal of continuous progress through the use of science and technology, toward a state of social perfection, was combined, not with a Religion of Humanity or a dictatorship of the proletariat, but with the economic doctrine of the free market and with the assumption of political power by industrial corporations. William Graham Sumner (1820–1903), teaching sociology and economics at Yale in the late nineteenth century, was the most influential critic of government regulation, labor unions, and political reform. It was through the free market and technological advance that humanity would make progress. Obviously this line of thinking has not lost its appeal in the English-speaking world even though the practical demands of modern technology require far more extensive governmental intervention in the economy than Spencer or Sumner would have envisioned in their worst nightmares.

But there is still a contrast between British and American constitutional ideas, even though they are essentially alike with respect to fundamental freedoms. As we have seen, the seventeenth-century dissenters in England and the Glorious Revolution of 1689 discredited the Divine Right of Kings, but the established church and the restored monarchy maintained through the eighteenth century the idea of sovereignty, supported by Edmund Burke's traditional theory of politics. In America, Adams and Franklin and Jefferson could start a federal republic with no established church, wildly dissenting faiths, and a conviction (at least among intellectual leaders) that the new scientific ways of thought were the guiding principles of a free constitutional system.

This approach went to the heart of the political issue, as James Wilson defined it. Wilson, born a Scot, was devoted to the Scottish "common-sense" philosophy which rejected Hume's empiricism that held human motivation was based on nothing but self-interest. As a member of the Supreme Court, in 1790 and 1791 he delivered lectures on law at the College of Philadelphia, in which he denied the validity of any royal sovereignty or ecclesiastical establishment and asserted that the "sovereign power of the society rests in the citizens at large," who should always be free to change their constitution whenever expedient. "The dread and redoubtable sovereign, when traced to his ultimate and genuine source, has been found, as he ought to have been found, in the free and independent man."[22]

In the United Kingdom, far more secular and skeptical in its attitude to religion than the United States, there is still the established church—indeed, there are two of them—headed by the monarch and ultimately controlled by the Parliament, and the establishment in England (though not in Scotland) still seeks in its doctrine to reestablish a formal connection with Catholicism. While the established church is still the traditional social bastion of Conservative politicians, the Labour party, officially sympathetic to socialism, remains rather more Methodist than Marxist in its social origins and popular support.

In the United States, where the religious denominations with the less affluent membership are the ones that insist on governmental action in support of their social views, there has never been as much support as in Britain for political control of industry. With no faith in the mystique of sovereignty, America is less willing to concede as much authority to any institutions in society and more eager to keep them—governmental and nongovernmental alike—under legalistic controls.

At this point, we may do well to get down off the high horse of philosophical speculation, and look at the ways in which different attitudes to authority have led to differences in the practical aspects of government administration.

IV

The Seamy Side of Sovereignty

While Great Britain and the United States have alike avoided totalitarian ideology in their politics, they have been forced to modify some of their old institutional habits in order to let their governments deal with the problems of contemporary technological society.

In order to make the work of government effective, historical traditions and constitutional theories have to be supported by systematic if not scientific methods of administration. The systems of personnel management, financial control, and government organization and procedures, however dreary their jargon may seem to the citizen, are what make constitutional systems tick. These aspects of the daily drudgery of government are the seamy side of sovereignty.

Over the past century, the United States has tried to improve its conduct of public business by imitating British institutions and procedures. The results have usually been generally beneficial but have often gone wrong in some important respect or have failed to measure up to the original intent of the reformers or to the model being imitated. It may be useful to consider why.

The influence of scientists and, before them, the religious dissenters may have been significant in this story. This is probably less because they had thought through any systematic political theory than because they had developed institutional habits suitable for running the affairs of churches or scientific societies or universities and then applied—or misapplied—them uncritically to governmental institutions.

If certain attitudes or habits of private institutions become pervasive in society, they may not be more important than formal constitutional structures, but they may still condition the ways in which those structures work. If we hope to understand the American political system better, it would help not only to compare it with the British, but also (if time and space and scholarly competence permitted) to see how other aspects of behavior in the two countries compare with each other.

Without making any such comparison in a comprehensive way, one might find it suggestive to observe the addiction of the two countries to football. It would be too subtle and profound a question to ask the political significance of the British preference for soccer— a flexible and fast-moving type of strategy, in which a single roster of players endures uninterrupted action for an entire game—over the rougher American football, with its elaborate system of rules, measurement of yardage, calculation of time-outs, and frequent substitutions of players. But one crude example may be given of the way in which the public reaction to the games illustrates national peculiarities.

In the United Kingdom, severe snowstorms in 1963 forced the national soccer league to cancel its matches. Most Americans tend to think of the British as sedate and polite and self-controlled and so are surprised at the vitriolic heckling of political speakers. They are even more surprised to learn that the crowds at soccer league games are bigger than sporting crowds in the United States, rather more passionate, and much more inclined to fist fights between those who bet on rival teams. Also they bet much more money, in national pools. So when all the matches were called off, what could be done? It was simple. A panel of experts was constituted, including former players, a manager, a referee, and (as chairman) Lord Brabazon of Tara. After solemn deliberation, they decided how each game would have come out if it had been played and what the result would have been. On the basis of those results the bets were settled.[1]

In the United States in 1977, the Washington Redskins football team played the St. Louis Cardinals in a game the Washington fans took very seriously. The Cardinals won, in part because of a controversial and disputed decision by the referee. A group of Washington fans thereupon filed a suit in federal court to have the referee's decision reversed by judicial decree.[2]

These two events are not the sort of thing that takes place regularly, even on their home turf. But it may seem to others as well as to me quite inconceivable that either of them could ever have happened on the other side of the Atlantic. For they typify attitudes to authority that differ substantially, and the difference may have a profound influence on the way public institutions operate. It is this conspicuous difference in public attitudes toward authority in general and governmental authority in particular that has limited the ability of American reformers to imitate British institutions and procedures. If we can understand how and why their reform efforts have been distorted, we might at least improve the ways in which we deal with problems at the administrative level in the future.

We might also learn more important lessons. Those who have proposed changes in the American Constitution in order to imitate the British parliamentary system will do well to ponder how much its apparent concentration of authority and coherence of policy at the Cabinet level are dependent on the substructure of systems of personnel, finance, and organization, and how dangerous it would be to graft the Cabinet-level constitutional structure onto the disorderly foundations of American congressional procedures and administrative practices. How far would America need to go in changing its administrative system in order to help top political authority achieve the political discipline and coherent policy that we attribute to British government?

It would be even more important to reflect on a more basic question: in view of the extent to which government pervades all aspects of society, would we sacrifice important values—especially in a large federal republic—by subjecting all policies to the control of a single tightly disciplined party, supported by an even more tightly disciplined civil service? Is it possible to make the American system more effective and accountable by more discriminating changes in our informal constitutional practices without changes in the written Constitution?

Before trying to face up to these more difficult questions, let us look more closely at the ways in which the fundamental administrative problems of American government appear at the levels of the departments and agencies of American government, as influenced by congressional committees. After this look at the seamy side of popular sovereignty, we may ask how similar problems have developed at the level of the Executive Office of the President—the White House and the cabinet. We may reserve for the final chapter the question how, under American conditions, we might undertake to improve both the efficiency and the democratic accountability of government.

The Career Civil Service

The first aspect of public administration on which the United States undertook to imitate the British is what, with scholarly propriety, we may call the bureaucracy. In popular usage, however, that term is not a scientific description but an insult. The British use it mainly to sneer at the career services on the Continent, while in America it is a slogan of political candidates who find it popular to campaign against the government.

A real bureaucracy is a career service heading the major departments of a government, with lifetime commitments and a common outlook or education and at least partly beyond political control. Some of the civil service reformers, whose model was the British service as reformed by Northcote and Trevelyan, wanted something like that for the U.S. when they advocated what became the Civil Service Act of 1883. But in the arguments over that act, Congress made sure that the reformers would get no such thing. It set the new merit system up in such a way as to make it impossible to imitate the key principles of the British system, which were designed to insure a tightly disciplined officer corps cutting across the upper levels of all the ministries and dedicated to lifetime careers. The new American merit system was designed to prevent the development of an elite corps and to make it possible for candidates to enter the service at any age. It forbade the creation of a separate category of officers for the higher grades and made it impossible to establish any educational requirements except, most significantly, in scientific or professional categories.[3] As a result, about two-thirds of the jobs in the top three grades of the service today are held by those who came up through scientific, professional, or specialized systems of education and governmental experience. Some have come in at senior levels from private employment, and more have their eyes on private jobs in the future.

To appreciate the effect of these prohibitions, which made impossible any disciplined coordination of policy, one may compare the U.S. civil service not only with the classic bureaucracies of Western Europe, but also with the U.S. army. For its general officers, the army needed not only West Point but also a jealously guarded system of postentry education and (after the 1921 National Security Act) a unified promotion list to maintain the domination of the generalists over the special arms and services.[4] The National Security Act was intended to make it possible to prepare a comprehensive strategy by unified staff work, at least within the army itself. It had not been easy to effect, in view of opposition from those bred in the old American tradition of reliance on the volunteer soldier, mobilized through the state militias.

It was much harder for Americans to give up their prejudice against establishments in civilian than in military personnel practices. The best way to avoid a bureaucracy, it seemed to personnel technicians as well as to politicians, was to maintain a system of personnel classification in which each job as a separate entity had its status, duties, and compensation defined by law. This apparently dull technical practice had profound political significance. Much as Calvinist doctrine a couple of centuries earlier rejected the authority of bishops and led to the control by local congregations over the careers of the clergy, the personnel classification system in practice put the status of the top civil service jobs at the mercy of market forces; in both cases it was then impossible to administer a hierarchical establishment, with systematic lifetime careers.

By 1935 those concerned with the failure of the higher civil service to respond to the challenges of the Depression and the New Deal realized that an overspecialized career service could not administer a coherent policy. The Commission of Inquiry on Public Service Personnel, a foundation-supported private committee, then recommended a new system with more adequate incentives for governmentwide loyalty among the overspecialized career officers. These ideas kept coming up, in one fashion or another, for more than forty years until they were partially enacted in the Civil Service Reform Act of 1978, creating a new Senior Executive Service. The new system proposed to give greater career rewards for service in the higher levels, to give more incentive to interdepartmental transfers to broaden experience, and to restrict the numbers of political appointments in the top grades. But it will have only limited effect as long as promotions are controlled by the several executive departments and agencies and they in turn are motivated by a constant desire to maintain the support of their counterparts among the congressional committees and constrained by the reluctance of each bureau's officers to admit outsiders into their ranks.

For in spite of the success of the Civil Service Reform Act of 1978 in changing the structure of the federal government's personnel system, the control over individual careers has not been effectively transferred to any central institution. That is not to belittle the change effected by that act. President Franklin Roosevelt had been handed one of his most notable defeats when the Congress labeled one of his reorganization efforts a "dictator bill," mainly because it proposed to substitute for the bipartisan Civil Service Commission a single-headed personnel agency, under the surveillance of a part-time watchdog committee to prevent political abuses. After Roosevelt several presidents made efforts in the same general direction, only to be rebuffed by Congress; so Carter's political success on this issue was striking. But it is not surprising that the President still lacks the authority to direct the personnel system to his own managerial taste[5] or to create an agency to manage the careers of senior civil service executives.

The contrast with the British civil service is a striking one, although since the Fulton Committee report a decade ago the British have been committed to opening the higher service up more generously to promotion from subordinate ranks and especially from the scientific and technical branches.[6] The most significant difference is that the civil service is not set up or controlled by legislative action; it remains Her Majesty's Service, and its organization, compensation, and all aspects of its personnel (except retirement) are controlled by executive action, normally dominated by the career officers themselves. Most important of all, the general spirit of the system is one of domination by the generalist over the specialist; the tradition of education in history and the classics, especially at Oxford and Cambridge, still gives cohesion to an officer corps that does not concede to the scientists any superiority in the understanding of policy.

The integration of policy is supported in Britain (and to almost the same extent in Canada) by two specific ways in which the career system is administered. Each civilian department, under the cabinet minister, is headed by a career civil servant (called in Canada a deputy minister) who is over all the constituent bureaus of the ministry. (In the U.S. the army's chief of staff plays such a role, but no career counterpart is permitted to occupy a position in the chain of hierarchical authority over all the bureaus of any civilian department.) The promotions of all higher civil servants are controlled, not by heads of the several ministries, but for the entire service by a top civil servant, who is responsible only to the Prime Minister and who is conceded by him a high degree of professional autonomy.

To those Americans who think of the parliamentary system as one of legislative supremacy, it may seem a paradox that the British parliament exerts no authority by legislation over the civil service, while the American separation of powers gives the President very little legal power over the personnel system of the so-called executive branch, however much his staff may control individual appointments. It is even more paradoxical that in Britain, even Conservative governments zealously defend the control by the civil service over significant aspects of the economy, while since the Second World War the most liberal American administrations have proceeded progressively to institute a system that, far from socializing the ownership of industry, has desocialized the functions of government itself: less than a tenth of the federal budget now goes to pay for the domestic programs directly administered by civil servants, while rather more goes to pay for programs contracted out to private institutions and as much again for work done by state and local officials. Five times as much goes to "entitlements," ranging from interest on the national debt to social security payments.[7]

The significance of these practices is not that they are merely convenient ways to delegate work for more efficient management to subsidiaries, as General Motors turns work over to Chevrolet or Buick. Each program is created by an independent political initiative and supported by some special political interest, which jealously insists on a degree of autonomy for its favorite program, usually with the help of a congressional committee. The delegation of public business to private institutions has recently taken place also in the United Kingdom through the use of "quasi-nongovernmental associations" popularly known as quangoes. But such institutions do not fit very well with the British idea of a clear-cut system of political accountability, and each one is seen as the potential nucleus of a special interest group. While American conservatives do not mind spending public resources as long as the spending is not controlled by the government, their British counterparts prefer to support the civil service rather than any private corporation to which its functions may be transferred by contractual arrangements. On the recommendation of a retired civil servant who believed that quangoes "may represent not only a spread of patronage but a concealed growth of government," Prime Minister Thatcher undertook to abolish as many quangoes as possible.[8]

In the United States the fragmentation in the political system that controls the personnel system is supported by the popular conviction that the role of the career civil servant is to administer efficiently the policies that have been enacted by Congress or ordered by the President but not to concern itself with the content of policy. That conviction has been supported by political scientists who cite as a precedent the nonpolitical status of the old Administrative Class of the British civil service. While its status was certainly nonpolitical, in that it was protected against patronage and committed to carrying out dutifully the orders of its political superiors, that class never pretended to stay out of policy issues; indeed, it always avowed publicly that its main duty was to deal with the substance of policy, especially to ensure its coordination among the various ministries, and its members never professed much interest in management in the American sense of that term.[9]

If Americans tried to draw an effective line between policy and administration, it was partly because scholars misread the British experience and partly because the civil service reformers needed a sales pitch to persuade politicians that the bureaucracy would not trespass on their powers. This effort to restrict the role of the career officer reflected the populist prejudice in favor of amateur leadership, a prejudice that continued in civil affairs long after the harsh realities of war made it impossible in the military services.

President Roosevelt's Committee on Administrative Management (the Brownlow Committee) tried in 1937 to fudge this issue, even though it clearly wanted the higher civil service to play important roles in the formulation or development of policy recommendations, by saying that its members should not occupy positions that were "policy determining" or "policy forming." This evasion did not persuade the second Hoover Commission (the Commission on Organization of the Executive Branch) in 1955; while it recommended the creation of a higher civil service of a more generalist nature, it tried to draw a sharp line between its public role, to be confined to its managerial responsibilities, and that of its political superiors, with exclusive responsibility for public advocacy. How the career officer could keep private any role in policy formulation, as long as congressional committees are free to question him about what he does and what he thinks, was not fully explained.[10]

So the American executive leaders have come to prefer amateur politicians in the upper reaches of their departmental management, while congressional committees are free to use scientists and technologists of all descriptions to help them control in detail the substance of policy. The new Senior Executive Service should help in the long run to bring about a greater degree of coherence in governmentwide policy and a stronger staff of generalists in the career system, but for its full realization, that hope is for a very long run indeed.

Money

Members of Congress like to remind themselves that the power of the purse was the weapon by which the representatives of the English people won control over the government and converted hereditary monarchy into a democracy. That is the way in which the United States remains within the historical tradition of English-speaking politics. They are less likely to emphasize another aspect of the British tradition: the power of the purse has been used for more than two centuries to impose tightly centralized control over the government as a whole. In the United States, by contrast, it has usually been used to support the dispersal of power and the disintegration of policy.

On the British side, the principle is clear. Constitutionally, no money may be appropriated except by vote of the House of Commons. Yet with equal constitutional effect, the way the House works is controlled by its own fundamental procedural rule, in effect ever since 1707: no money may be appropriated that has not first been requested by the Crown, which in effect means the Government of the Day—the Cabinet under the leadership of the Prime Minister. (In Canada and Australia, the same principle is written into their constitutions: the Governor in Council must request any funds which the parliament is to appropriate, and this means in practical terms a united action by the Cabinet, under the leadership of the Prime Minister.) After funds are appropriated, the Government of the Day is under no legal obligation to spend them. Under such arrangements, as long as the Cabinet is collectively responsible to the House of Commons, there is no practical political way for special interest groups to use appropriation acts to push for the kind of influence that in the United States is exercised through appropriations subcommittees.[11] The tight unity of this system is supported by the fact that the comptroller and auditor general, who reviews expenditures for regularity for the House of Commons, has no power to hold up expenditures but only to report on them after they are made. It is further confirmed by the arrangement made in the early 1920s that the position of the accounting officer for each ministry, on whose work the comptroller and auditor general must pass, is always held by the permanent secretary—the top administrative civil servant—of the ministry.[12]

In the early days of the American republic, Alexander Hamilton's hopes for a strong central finance authority failed to prevail, less because Congress was against the executive than because the President wanted (or needed) to rely more on his political connections with members of Congress than on his limited Constitutional authority. Thomas Jefferson recommended in his first annual message to Congress the appropriation of "specific sums to every specific purpose susceptible of definition," and with the help of Secretary of the Treasury Gallatin encouraged the "line item" appropriations that still distinguish the financial system of the United States from those of other nations.[13] Control of details rather than of broad policy then became characteristic of the tactics of "progressive" reformers. The result has been not to strengthen the coherence of public policy and political discipline but rather to multiply some specific forms of control over pieces of the executive by different congressional committees.

The process of control over the spending of money always involved two steps: legislation to authorize a function or program, and the appropriation of money to support it. In the late nineteenth century these two processes were often combined in a single committee; the Commerce Committee of the House, for example, got control over the appropriations bill for rivers and harbors in 1879, and shortly thereafter the most tempting programs—agriculture, army, navy, Indian affairs, and foreign affairs—were separated from any single financial discipline and controlled by the specialized committees.[14]

The resulting waste and political patronage led reformers, impressed by the financial reforms led by Gladstone and others in the United Kingdom, to begin to argue in the 1880s for a centralized budget system for the United States. President Taft set up the Commission on Economy and Efficiency in 1911. The report of that commission, relying heavily on the British experience with financial management, was influential in the plan that was finally set up by the Budget and Accounting Act of 1921. The act not only created a Budget Bureau for the executive and a General Accounting Office as a congressional "watchdog," but in each house of Congress restored the authority of the Appropriations Committee over the entire executive budget.[15] The budget process was then made twofold: each program first needed authorizing legislation proposed by a legislative committee and then an appropriation act controlled by appropriations committees and subcommittees. The normal practice (except for the subject that was the overwhelming political temptation, rivers and harbors) was by legislation to authorize each main function on a permanent basis with no precise dollar figures. This, however, gave the legislative committees too little separate influence and later, after the Second World War, they began to require a new statute authorizing a specific dollar level of expenditures each year for each program, while the appropriations subcommittees continued to take separate action, sometimes refusing to provide the funds for programs mandated by law.

A third form of control is exercised by personnel ceilings, setting limits on the numbers of employees and sometimes on the numbers in specific ranks or grades; the agency that finds itself with more money than freedom to make appointments is then induced to contract out to private institutions the administration of publicly financed programs.

The budget as a tool of central control is then greatly weakened not only by the deliberate dispersal of authority within the Congress, but also by the invention of other ways of supporting programs. Tax exemptions for programs carried on by private corporations and regulations to require them to perform public functions, along with the system of grants to state and local governments and contracts with private institutions, have added to the complexity of public business. Herbert Hoover used to remark sourly that the U.S. had not socialized private business by taking over its ownership but only (through the income tax) by taking away its income. He might well have gone on to observe that the government had decided not to own business because it was easier and more flexible to rent it through contractual arrangements or to control it through regulation. The budget is no longer the comprehensive tool controlling the entire range of government programs that it was expected to be when it was first established.

While the budget is nevertheless an indispensable tool of management for the President, its efficacy in restraining spending depends, not on the President's legal or Constitutional authority, but only on his political influence at any given time. While the House of Commons cannot appropriate money that the Prime Minister has not requested, Congress considers itself free in both law and practice to appropriate money that the President has not requested and then to force him to spend it. In resentment against President Nixon's stretching of his limited legal authority, the Congress, by an elaborate statutory process, took away the President's former ability to "impound" appropriated funds that he found it unnecessary or unwise to spend. But it is not merely that the President must spend money that Congress may on its own initiative appropriate. Perhaps more of a constraint is the political necessity of asking for what he does not want. The President, in order to bargain for legislative support for the programs he likes, must continue to put in his budget money for programs he does not like and then tolerate control by congressional committees of the way in which it is spent.

The same desire to restrict the President that constrained his power of impoundment also led to what seemed at first an even more powerful assault on executive leadership. The President had gained power by being given a budget office, so the argument ran; so why should not Congress regain its authority by having a congressional budget office of its own? It set one up in 1974, along with a budget committee for each house (on top of the existing appropriations committees and subcommittees), and a procedure by which it obliged itself to reconcile its several taxing and spending acts with one another into a single binding comprehensive policy.

For several years the procedure seemed ineffective, but by 1981 President Reagan's popular leadership produced an apparently paradoxical result. An act that was expected to strengthen the power of the purse and help the Congress control the executive turned out to be a powerful tool of presidential leadership. Since the act made it possible, by its "reconciliation" procedure, to impose effective discipline on the disintegrating competition of federal bureaus and congressional committees in league with each other against any comprehensive leadership, it began to seem more to the advantage of the President than of the Congress.

Senators and representatives who resent any central political leadership or discipline, even from within the Congress, like it no better even if such leadership is exercised through a process which Congress had enacted in order to restrain presidential influence. Perhaps the rivalry of the Congress with the President is actually less significant than the conflict in both branches between the forces of disintegration and the rather weak efforts to integrate public policies.

Organization

The term *branch*, however, is a misleading metaphor. Organization charts and television pundits to the contrary, there is no such thing as an executive branch of the U.S. government. The Constitution gives the President certain executive powers, but it does not mention an executive branch. Instead it lets the Congress by legislation set up executive departments and control their organization and procedures to any degree it likes.

To some of the leaders of the Constitutional Convention who feared legislative more than executive encroachment, this was a mistake. John Adams predicted gloomily that, because the Constitution gave the President only a limited, rather than an absolute, veto power over legislation, it was inevitable that the President would be deprived of his proper authority by congressional usurpation.[16] Beginning with the Jeffersonian era, the habit of enacting detailed statutory controls over matters of organization as well as finance and of putting bureau chiefs more under the control of congressional committees than of their departmental secretaries spread, until by the late nineteenth century the presidency was, in its lack of authority over organization and administration, the weak institution that Woodrow Wilson described in his *Congressional Government*.

The contrast that Wilson drew with the British system is now less sharp but still generally holds. The ministries of state in Britain may be established by statute, but the statutes are bare summaries that leave the internal structure and procedures of each ministry to executive discretion. The freedom of the Cabinet to create new agencies, abolish old ones, and distribute their functions is rarely challenged. When the U.S. undertook to set up an agency after the Second World War to control atomic energy, Congress took many months to debate the issue, produced several volumes of testimony, and ended with a highly detailed statute. The British set their agency up when the executive notified the Commons that it was publicly formalizing a system that it had previously created by confidential and informal action.

Congress, however, in matters of organization as well as in personnel and finance, decided largely on its own initiative that a greater measure of central discipline was needed and that the President ought to be conceded a bit more opportunity for leadership. It grudgingly granted President Hoover the right to reorganize in a limited way by executive orders that would be subject to veto by either House of Congress; his proposed orders in 1932 were all vetoed.

A more effective reorganization procedure was set up in 1939, following the recommendations of President Roosevelt's Committee on Administrative Management. Two of the three members of that committee, Louis Brownlow and Charles E. Merriam, had spent some time in England in 1936 studying the British system of organization.[17] They had also commissioned Professors William Y. Elliott of Harvard and Lindsay Rogers of Columbia to study the central executive institutions of Britain and other European governments.

The approach of the President's committee owed a great deal to the British precedents, especially to the theory of delegated legislation and legislative review of executive orders. But after the committee's recommendations had been voted down in 1937, a new procedure was invented not by its members, but by congressional staff: the device of Reorganization Plans, subject to congressional veto, that would have full statutory effect. This procedure became law in the series of Reorganization Acts, beginning in 1939 under Roosevelt, and extended as a result of the recommendations of the two Hoover commissions in 1948 and 1954.[18] Those acts gave the President the right to propose Reorganization Plans subject to congressional veto and (as subsequently reenacted with modifications) became the basis of a series of reorganizations through the Carter administration, generally with the purpose of reducing the statutory independence of subordinate bureaus, boards, and commissions, and strengthening the responsibility of the President and his department heads.

As time went on, however, the results suggested that it made less difference than had been hoped to put a bureau chief legally under the authority of a department head: the fragmentation of executive authority is not fundamentally the result of the formal Constitutional or legal structure. Congressional committees and subcommittees, relying on the continuous need of career officers for annual renewal of statutory authority and appropriations, reasserted their control, overriding that of the so-called cabinet officer, by informal understandings, made explicit in committee hearings and recorded in the legislative history.

Legislative Organization and Procedures

The root of these differences between the American and British systems is in the procedures by which the legislature does business and its members are chosen. In the United Kingdom, the House of Commons has, in theory, the ultimate power as against the Cabinet but, in practice, exercises it only through the ministers of the Crown. Could members of the House do otherwise? Could they, as members of the Chamber of Deputies of the Third French Republic were doing a half century ago, organize legislative committees apart from the Cabinet and take effective control of pieces of government business? So far they have not done so: the custom that party leaders, after long indoctrination in the traditions of the House of Commons, become lifetime members of H.M. Privy Council and share its legal obligations of secrecy and loyalty to the Crown has prevented the House from destroying the unity of a monarchy and substituting the lack of discipline that is customary in republics.

There are current tendencies in that direction that seem dangerous to many British politicians: the decline in the power of the whips to compel party regularity in voting in the House, the recent creation of committees of the House with specialized areas of oversight, the provision to them of staff assistance, and the proposal that the nomination of members and the selection of ministers be shared by members of the Labour party in the House of Commons with party members outside the House, especially in the trade unions. It was the fear of this sharing of control with the unions that led several leaders of the Labour party to secede to form the new Social Democratic party. It was a fear that had deeper roots than the normal greed of politicians for power, for it was supported by the constitutional faith that power and responsibility must go together, and ultimate power over the choice of the rulers must rest with the elected members of Parliament.

While the British may see these developments as radical changes, from the American perspective it seems that neither outside party influence nor the new committees are likely to break up the disciplined responsibility of the British Cabinet. The Cabinet still retains substantial control over the agenda of the House of Commons. The committees of the House can have staff members only in small numbers, usually as assigned to them by the head of the civil service. (In Canada, the research staff members of the house are assigned, not to the specialized committees and not to individual members, but to the party caucuses.) The committees do not challenge the Cabinet on any issue of major policy, as the Cabinet may define it, by demanding that the Commons vote on the issue. They cannot question civil servants about their personal opinions on issues of policy. While they may now be informed about the titles of the principal committees of the Cabinet, the Prime Minister refuses to give them information about the terms of reference of those committees or their membership.[19] Canada is more open; it publishes the titles and membership of Cabinet committees. As Samuel H. Beer noted, after reviewing the recent tremendous decline in the central authority of party leadership in his *Britain Against Itself*, it is nevertheless still true that "to their relief the British may be informed that the Americanization of their politics is still far from complete."[20]

It is not surprising that the more ambitious young members of the House of Commons are not yet inclined to look on the chairmanship of one of the House committees as a position of real power but are inclined instead to behave in those committees in ways calculated to earn them appointment as parliamentary secretaries or junior ministers.

The Cabinet itself is supported in its collective responsibility by the tight unity of the higher civil service. Indeed some former Cabinet members complain about their inability, as heads of individual ministries, to penetrate the corporate identity of the permanent heads of their departments. Some of the ministers are inclined to think that they should have more of a voice in the appointment of their principal career subordinates, the permanent secretaries and under-secretaries, who are chosen by the Prime Minister with the advice of the top career officer, the secretary of the Cabinet, whose staff manages the system of careers of the higher civil service and advises on government organization. (Essentially the same system prevails in Canada.) Prime Minister Thatcher reestablished this system in 1981, after a thirteen-year interlude during which a career officer other than the Cabinet secretary had headed the Civil Service Department. She took this action by an order in council, assuming for herself the position of minister for the civil service and making the cabinet secretary also the permanent secretary of the Management and Personnel Office. No legislative action was required or expected. The contrast with the painfully extended congressional debate over the Civil Service Reform Act of 1978 is an illuminating one.[21]

This system obviously gives great influence over policy as well as administration to the career officers who serve as permanent secretaries of the various ministries. Under it, an occasional minister may argue plaintively that he ought to be permitted, as he had not been, to sit in at the meetings of the interdepartmental committees of permanent officials who presented him customarily with completed staff work which made it very hard for him to do more than say yes or no. Extensive complaints of the same nature may be found in the three volumes of the diaries of Richard Crossman and in his book *The Myths of Cabinet Government*. But an American observer may well wonder whether, if the administrative procedures by which the civil service defends the unity of government policy were opened up to control by ministers and junior ministers, they would not soon be taken away from the Cabinet by other committees of the House, and wind up in a state of American-style disintegration.[22]

For the role of the civil service establishment in Great Britain and Canada is more than that of a mere bureaucracy, managing the programs enacted by the legislature. It is in one specific and significant way conceded authority at the crux of political conflict, with responsibility for helping to maintain the balance of power among the parties and between them and the permanent government. Its most delicate responsibility comes when one party defeats another and takes control of the government. At such a time of political transition, some way must be found to keep the new government from using the files and documents of the previous government for partisan advantage. The United States does so by setting up a new institution, the presidential library, built with private funds, to serve as the custodian of the papers of the outgoing President and his associates, with the right of restricting access to those documents. The British do it more simply: in the normal course of business, the secretary of the Cabinet, a career civil servant, tells the new Prime Minister and Cabinet which papers in the official files they may see and which they may not.

The Cabinet secretary does so, of course, not because he has authority vested in him by statute, but because he is accepted in normal cases as the arbiter of a convention agreed to by all parties as a political principle. In an exceptionally difficult issue, however, the secretary may have to appeal to the authority of the previous Prime Minister in refusing to release his era's documents. For example, in the review proposed in 1982 by Prime Minister Margaret Thatcher of the events leading up to the Argentine invasion of the Falklands, former Prime Minister Heath, from an earlier Conservative government, as well as former Labour Prime Minister Callaghan, energetically complained that Thatcher had no right to see the documents from their previous administrations. She promptly conceded and instead proposed a committee of inquiry to be made up of six members of the Privy Council no longer in active office so that "no member of the present Government can or will see any documents of any previous administration unless he or she was a member of such an administration and is entitled for that reason to see those papers."[23] This episode merely illustrates the outer boundary of the Cabinet secretary's role, which normally goes unquestioned as an essential safeguard of the constitutional system. In Canada, it is harder to rely entirely on tradition and custom to give such authority to the Cabinet secretary (the clerk of the Privy Council), who is accordingly given a similar role by explicit statutory enactment.[24]

Countries that have had republican revolutions may continue to support strong bureaucracies, as France and Germany demonstrate. But as long as a bureaucracy is merely the servant of elected politicians, it is hard for it to maintain a firm status of impartiality, so that the system can tolerate periodic changes in party control. This tolerance is becoming more difficult in Great Britain as the Labour party drifts toward an effort to control the Cabinet from outside the Parliament, where the traditions of the monarchy, with its balance between the elected politicians and the career establishment, may not be respected. But up to the present, the system has worked, maintaining its unification of powers on a monarchical principle with the most effective separation of the functions of legislation and administration known in any free society.

The fundamental monarchical principle is that the King can do no wrong. That does not mean, of course, that as a person he is good. It only means that political and legal action to correct his crimes or mistakes must, in order to protect the continuity of the constitutional system, be directed at his responsible ministers. In a legal sense, this principle applies to the monarch as a person; in a more important political sense, it applies to the establishment that serves him—His Majesty's Civil Service. The British parliamentary system can work because the House of Commons continues, in the main, to hold the ministers responsible for administrative actions and to refrain from questioning the civil servants about their views on policies.

The fundamental principle of the American republic is the opposite: the President can do no right. He can of course receive unlimited adulation, and sometimes gain tremendous political support. But there is no constitutional procedure by which, after he states a policy that he thinks is right, he can get the Congress clearly to say he is right. He cannot expect the Congress to approve or reject his program as a whole, rather than amending it out of all recognition, or (even after approval) be sure he can execute it without having it sabotaged by detailed legislative committee controls over organization, personnel, or financial procedure.

For Congress is a collective noun, not a disciplined entity. The real power is in the subcommittees, some five hundred of them. In recent years the subcommittees have won the right to employ their own staffs. The staffs to the committees and their subcommittees and members now number some twenty thousand. The political ambition of the members and staff members is not to become heads of executive departments but to make the most of the specialized functions over which they have oversight. As chairmen, they gain far longer experience and depth of knowledge of executive business than the secretaries or assistant secretaries of the departments, who average less than two years in tenure. And they are less interested in the general policies of their party leaders than in their own control of specialized program administration, exercised under the euphemism of "oversight."[25] The Carter White House staff, struggling to exercise some party leadership, was dismayed to find that, out of 334 Democrats in the two houses, there were only about two dozen who did not enjoy the independent power that comes from chairing some committee or subcommittee.[26]

The influence of subcommittee and committee leaders over specialized programs at the expense of governmentwide policy or party unity is made possible by their right to deal directly with civil servants on policy issues. Such collusion then extends to the private interest groups affected, and the collaboration among congressional committees, bureau officials, and lobbyists—the notorious "iron triangle"—is the main obstacle to the unity of each political party and to any administrative discipline over the higher civil service.

But the strength of the "iron triangle" does not depend on organization and procedure. It rests more fundamentally on what American politicians and the public generally believe in. They do not believe in letting political leaders have the authority to make important decisions on the basis of their value judgments. They prefer an approach that is partly scientistic and partly legalistic.

As for the scientistic side, the members of Congress expect career officers who have scientific or professional backgrounds to give their opinions publicly as experts on major policy issues, regardless of the policies of their superiors. And if they fail to get the right answers, they turn as well to outside scientific testimony. In the decade before 1981, Congress, by more than thirty statutes, assigned to the National Academy of Sciences the task of recommending the answers (or checking the answers provided by official agencies) to such broad policy questions as the proper extent of regulatory controls over the environment or the need for new federal programs in international health or a review of the main changes in the program of the National Aeronautics and Space Administration.

Since they cannot control the administration by hiring and firing its officials, they resort instead to giving it highly detailed directions, either through the informal "legislative history" of committee hearings or through detailed statutes, which in turn require detailed regulations. For example, in 1975 Congress enacted the "Education for All Handicapped Children Act." In that statute, twenty-two pages were devoted to specifying in detail the types of services to be assured through grants to state and local governments. The law required that the local administrator develop for each handicapped child a special statement of program based on five specified types of information and that reports on such programs be made to the House and Senate committees. The regulations by the Department of Health, Education, and Welfare that were required by that legislation took up 130 pages in the *Code of Federal Regulations* and were, one may suppose, blamed on the power-hungry bureaucracy not only by journalistic pundits but also by members of Congress other than those responsible for the statute that required them.[27]

The effort to bring such detailed provisions under the control of some general standards of policy then takes two forms: control by the judiciary, and the "legislative veto" by the Congress.

The failure of the Congress and the President to face up to general policy issues leads the American judiciary to assume control in ways that frighten many legal authorities. Statutes which make the government morally and legally responsible for sweeping reforms without the appropriations or the administrative competence to fulfill them require American courts to give detailed instructions to local administrators regarding such issues as the size of prison cells or the busing of school children but often without the practical capacity to back up their decisions.

The failure of the Congress either to define its purposes precisely in statutes or to entrust the executive agency with enough discretion to put them into effect also leads to the effort to control detailed administration by the "legislative veto." This is the procedure by which the Congress, as it grants money or authority to a department, provides that it may not be used in any way the Congress or one of its committees subsequently disapproves. For more than a half century Presidents and attorneys general have argued that such legislative vetoes are unconstitutional. But this issue, too, can hardly be settled by legalistic arguments. An agency that wants money for specific projects from an appropriations subcommittee is likely, no matter what the attorney general thinks, to want to assure members of that subcommittee that it will respect their views regarding the selection of the projects.[28]

In the selection of specific projects, especially those involving various types of public works, the interaction between executive agencies and congressional committees is so intimate that it is hard to think about the process in terms of Constitutional provisions governing the relations of the Congress to the President. Neither the Congress as a whole nor the President personally has very much to do with the business. Several presidents since World War II, following the recommendations of their attorneys general, have objected to various forms of the legislative veto over specific executive actions. But usually such legislative vetoes did little more than formally ratify the exercise of actual administrative control by congressional committees over administrative bureaus or divisions. In several statutes the Constitutional issue was evaded entirely by provisions which did not undertake to say how the Congress or any part of it should act to control any part of the executive. Instead, they simply prescribed, as Congress has every legal right to do, the internal procedure of the Congress. One such prescription required that the appropriations committees could not consider any appropriation for a watershed protection or flood control project or for the construction of a new public building, unless the specific project in question first had the approval of the appropriate legislative committee.[29]

The moral of this episode was that the letter of the Constitution is no protection for the President if the Congress wishes to use the power of the purse, not to affirm the unity of the executive as the British House of Commons had customarily done, but instead to parcel it out in small bits and pieces among the subcommittees and staff. It is at just this level of formality—an internal rule of house procedure—by which the House of Commons has maintained since

1707 the fundamental principle of the parliamentary cabinet system: appropriate no funds except those requested by H.M. Government. John Adams understated the problem: an absolute veto for the President could not have been maintained, any more than the legal veto power of the King, once the Congress began to use the power of the purse as a bargaining lever.

One may argue, as those who propose to imitate the parliamentary system often do, that Congress refuses to delegate to the President and resorts to these excessively legalistic forms of control because it cannot control the tenure of the executive and therefore considers it a rival power rather than a faithful servant. That argument, however, is complicated by the fact that, even within its own affairs, the Congress does not operate as a disciplined unit.

The most generally ignored but important fact is that no parliamentary system can operate with a cabinet responsible to a legislative body unless the power to control the tenure of the executive is concentrated in a single house. At the time when Wilson wrote *Congressional Government* the Senate was in disrepute as an undemocratic institution, its members elected by the state legislatures. It was therefore not ridiculous to assume that its legitimacy as an equal power would decline, and the House under an aggressive Speaker would become a disciplined body that would continue to take over actual power, making the President into a ceremonial Constitutional monarch. But in 1913 when the Seventeenth Amendment provided for the direct election of the Senate and thus made it an equally legitimate voice of the people, it became clear that the Congress could never speak with a single voice in its relation with either the executive or the electorate.

The multiplicity of congressional controls greatly complicates the administrative problem of the executive. But it is more significant that it reduces the capacity of the Congress as a whole, under any system of internal political leadership, to impose some coherence of policy over its competing committees and subcommittees. If Congress cannot control the executive, the fundamental reason is that it prefers not to control itself.

The growing strength of special interest groups and the decline of the parties are conventionally blamed for these disintegrating tendencies. But that decline itself requires explanation. One suggestion is the loss of party patronage as the glue of party loyalty. But patronage was never the kind of glue that held votes together in support of policies and programs or of effective presidential leadership; it held them together mainly for the purpose of grabbing more patronage. As the old Washington joke put it, by every patronage appointment the President creates nine enemies and one ingrate. For as John C. Calhoun argued more than a century ago, it takes a country with a monarchy and peerage to make patronage serve as a support for central authority, rather than a temptation to political insubordination.[30] This was true of the old retail form of patronage in individual jobs; it is even more true of the new wholesale patronage that comes with contracting government functions out in wholesale style to private corporations, which can pay their officers higher salaries without anyone noticing that they too are "tax-eaters."

The breakdown of party discipline in the Congress, such as it was, is the result of more fundamental social changes. The instant reporting of detailed issues by television; its public exposure of the opinions of civil servants as well as politicians; the Freedom of Information Act, which has opened up the policy councils of government in practice less to the general public than to lobbyists and special interests; and above all the changes in the nominating system, with primaries replacing party caucuses as the road to power—all these would make it hard to change the system as a whole in order to respond to unified policy leadership rather than specialized interests. For they add up to a set of attitudes about democratic responsibility that denies the moral right of a disciplined party to make compromises among competing values and especially to do so by confidential procedures.

Two qualifications to these sweeping generalizations are in order. The British are showing some slight signs of moving in the American direction by loosening up their party discipline, relaxing their secrecy, and bringing more specialists into the top administrative ranks. On the American side, Congress has responded to appeals (or acted on its own initiative) to strengthen the presidency or its own forces of coordination in various ways over the past half century, most notably in recent years by the creation of the Senior Executive Service and the Congressional Budget Office.

The difficulties that the United States has been encountering in its effort to bring greater coherence and responsibility into its systems of personnel, finance, and organization have been matched at the apex of political authority by the experience of the Executive Office of the President since it was established in 1939. To that experience we turn in the next chapter.

V

The Institutional Presidency and the Cabinet

The most comprehensive effort to overcome the fragmentation of policies and programs that we have been discussing was the creation, nearly a half century ago, of the Executive Office of the President. Since that time, the Executive Office has grown much more in size and power than originally intended, but at the sacrifice of its fundamental principles.

Those principles had been intended to provide a healthy balance between the authority of the President and his accountability to the Congress as a whole and another appropriate balance within the executive between the responsibility of the department heads—often misleadingly labeled "cabinet government"—and the President's reliance on his staff in the White House and other parts of the Executive Office.

Bipartisan support for such a balanced approach seemed possible just after the first decade of the Executive Office. Its creation had been recommended by President Roosevelt's Committee on Administrative Management, headed by Louis Brownlow.[1] In anti-Roosevelt circles, it remained suspect as a New Deal innovation until it was confirmed in 1949 as a regular part of the constitutional system by the Commission on the Organization of the Executive Branch, headed by former President Hoover.[2]

The fact that a populist Democrat like Louis Brownlow and a conservative Republican like Herbert Hoover could agree on this innovation seemed to suggest that a bipartisan consensus could be developed on the nature and purpose of the President's staff agencies and on his use of cabinet committees. Brownlow had helped FDR subordinate his delight in disorder to the conviction that New Deal purposes would suffer if not administered on a more orderly basis; Hoover had rejected the attitudes of the Republican congressional leadership and insisted on a strong presidency, with its staff support and cabinet organized according to principles very much like those that the Brownlow Committee had recommended.

The press reports and political debates did not reflect those principles with any fair balance when they were first outlined in 1937 by the Brownlow Committee. The headlines concentrated on the phrase used in the committee report to describe the qualifications of the White House staff, including "a passion for anonymity," a phrase which Brownlow had picked up from Tom Jones, who had been secretary to three British prime ministers, Lloyd George, MacDonald, and Baldwin. The political debates turned heavily on the creation of the several staff agencies in the new Executive Office, and paid little attention to the more important (but less specific) principles that were recommended with respect to the reduction in the number of executive departments and agencies, the delegation to their heads of more effective authority over their subordinates and hence a better opportunity to serve as policy advisers to the President, and their accountability to the Congress.

When the Executive Office was finally established in 1939, it included the Bureau of the Budget (transferred from the Treasury, where, following the British precedent, it had been set up in 1921); institutions for planning, personnel management, public information, and emergency management; and an inner White House Office with six personal assistants.

The new institutions were staff agencies, but the main principles on which they were based were designed to keep them from encroaching on the roles of the secretaries of the executive departments. For all these staffs were expected to conform to four principles: first, they were to help the President but not to have any authority in their own right, nor to be in a chain of command to the heads of executive departments; second, they were to deal only with issues of such importance to the President that they could not be delegated to the department heads; third, the department heads, not members of the Executive Office, were to be the President's principal lieutenants and accountable to the Congress; and fourth, except for the White House staff and the heads of the institutional agencies, the Executive Office was to be staffed on a career and merit basis.

Since then, however, as the Executive Office has grown, its original principles, even though reaffirmed by most subsequent official studies, have been abandoned in practice. The total personnel of the Executive Office has doubled since World War II, and the number with political appointments indicating direct access to the President has increased at a much higher rate.[3] Cabinet members complain of being pushed around by Executive Office staff, who are the darlings of the television commentators and the targets of Washington lobbyists. And members and committees of Congress sometimes attack the staff agencies and the cabinet committees and sometimes thrust unwanted responsibilities on them, all the while seeking to reduce the discretionary flexibility with which the President may organize and use them.

As a result the system lacks the coherence which is the goal of a good staff system. The purpose of a presidential staff is not to duplicate the work of the department heads (the cabinet members) and their staffs. If it becomes too large or too specialized, it defeats its own purpose, and the President simply has another bureaucratic obstacle to deal with.

Moreover, the system then lacks the responsibility which is the goal of a good departmental structure. If departments come to be ordered about by staff operating from the political shelter of the White House, the department heads can no longer be truly responsible for the duties which are assigned them by statute, nor can they participate effectively with their cabinet colleagues in advising the President on long-range policies of common interest, or defending those policies before the Congress.

These distortions in the development of the Executive Office show the difficulty of imitating administrative institutions from another culture, especially one that is accustomed to accept a quite different degree of authority in its top leadership. The proposals for strengthening the presidency owed something to the imitation of each of three models, all in cultures different from the civilian side of American government.

First, there was the perennial idea that had supported earlier reorganization in state and municipal as well as the federal government: for more economy and efficiency, government should be run more like private business.

Second, Brownlow and his colleagues (Charles E. Merriam and Luther Gulick) had been influenced by the study that they had made of the British administrative system and especially of the Cabinet office in the summer of 1936, and they were of course aware of the earlier studies on which the U.S. had based its reforms in the fields of personnel and finance.

Third, there was the one aspect of American government in which—even if spasmodically—a certain respect was accorded to authority, namely, the military. In military affairs, the hard lesson had been learned that leadership cannot be provided by inspired amateurs alone but that coherence and responsibility in both policy and management depend on a system of organization and professionalized personnel. For the civilian side of the government, this understanding came a generation later. Even in the military, it had taken a long time to get over the notion that leadership meant riding a horse at the head of a charge into battle. Washington and Jackson and Zachary Taylor, U. S. Grant and Theodore Roosevelt, became popular heroes and Presidents on the strength of that myth. But it played out after the Spanish American War, largely because the professionals were less impressed by the Rough Riders' cavalry glamor than by the disastrous muddles in logistics and sanitation that proved the nation's incapacity to fight a war against a modern military power.

The military were to continue to make substantial contributions to the development of the presidency as an institution. General Pershing's finance officer for the American Expeditionary Force in France, Charles G. Dawes, a reserve general, came home to head the first important presidential staff agency, the Bureau of the Budget, which as we have seen was in 1921 tucked away in the Treasury Department for protective coloration. And after World War II it was two career generals whose talents were less in combat leadership than in diplomacy and organization—George C. Marshall and Dwight D. Eisenhower—who groped for ways to convert the system of co-ordination that had given the grand alliance a measure of unity into a civilian system for the guidance of the American government as a whole.

Like those of the Brownlow Committee a decade earlier, the ideas of General Marshall and General Eisenhower were derived in part from their observation of the British system. Their approach differed in one important way from that of the Brownlow Committee: as military leaders, they were—it may seem paradoxical to note—less in favor of executive discretion and more inclined to want to base their system for top coordination of the government on an explicit set of congressional enactments.

It may now be useful to consider how this difference of outlook and other political complications have made it hard to develop for the presidency both a small generalist staff in the Executive Office, and an effective system of consultation with the cabinet and its committees. Let us take these two aspects of the problem up in turn.

The Degradation of the Generalist Staff Principle

The goal of creating a small generalist staff has clearly been muddled since the Executive Office was established by a varied series of steps. A career administrator is tempted to blame them on congressional politics, but a detached observer might well conclude that the blame should fall equally on Congress (including its committees and staff) and on the presidency (including the President's staff), both being motivated by short-run political advantage more than the commitment to build a sound institution over the long pull. These steps may be described in four categories.

SPECIAL OPERATIONAL PURPOSES

Since it was obvious that agencies within the Executive Office, even if they had no statutory power in their own right, enjoyed special influence because of their proximity to the President, special interests within and outside the Congress saw opportunities to push particular programs in one direction or another by basing them in the

Executive Office.[4] The purpose of such agencies might be to enhance a program or, on the other hand, to reduce the independent influence of particular executive departments. Such tactics accounted, for example, for the creation of the Office of Drug Abuse Policy and the Office of Economic Opportunity. Then there were cases in which the President tried to transfer particular responsibilities of a comparatively routine nature out of the Executive Office, and Congress—eager to pin any blame on him personally—by control of appropriations, insisted on their return. For example, the President tried in 1973 to shift from his Budget Office to the General Services Administration various routine functions relating to cash management and data processing, but Congress withheld funds until they were returned.[5]

It is very hard to tell whether a congressional initiative put an inappropriate operation inside the Executive Office or whether the President took the initiative in order to get political support or avoid difficulty in choosing between competing departments. For example, President Kennedy set up the Special Representative for Trade Negotiations inside the Executive Office in 1962 in order to avoid having to choose between the State and Commerce Departments and their respective backers within the Congress. (Faced with a similar problem more recently, Canada considered putting its Trade Department in the Cabinet Office, in order to avoid offending the ministries of finance and of commerce, but on principle finally located it in External Affairs.) Or somewhat earlier, President Truman appointed in the White House a special representative on food policy in order to give his own international approach greater freedom from the domestic interests of the Department of Agriculture.

If it was a violation of the original principles of the Brownlow Committee to put operating agencies in the Executive Office, the first offense was that of Brownlow himself. By Executive Order 8248, which he helped draft for President Roosevelt, the Office for Emergency Management was set up as a legal fiction—a convenient umbrella under which wartime emergency agencies could be established by flexible executive action. Within the OEM were established the War Production Board, the Office of Scientific Research and Development, and all the other major civilian agencies for the prosecution of the war. The violation of principles was taken to be justified by the emergency, and the OEM agencies were all abolished after the war. But exceptional cases have a way of becoming routine operations; so the later overloading of the Executive Office with operating functions seems to have been inevitable.

THE SALES PITCH CORRUPTS THE PURPOSE

The original purpose of providing the President with high quality staff work on the great issues of the present and future was clearly degraded as the Executive Office (and especially the Bureau of the Budget) came to be overloaded with routine duties and specific managerial details. On this issue, it is tempting, and partly true, to argue that the basic principles of the Executive Office were distorted because the purposes for which Brownlow and Hoover wanted them were less influential in determining the outcome than the sales pitch that their followers in what came to be called the public administration movement felt obliged to employ.[6] The Brownlow Committee, by virtue of its report to the President, assumed the leadership of that general movement that had been built up during the 1920s, mainly in state and municipal government, for political reform and managerial efficiency. Even though the report of the committee and the individual writings of its members explicitly disagreed with several of its major emphases, the momentum of its general sales pitch colored the way in which their report was read.

That sales pitch, in its crude form, depended on two ideas. Taxpayers' associations and chambers of commerce argued that efficiency and economy in government were the main purposes of government reform and that these depended on imitating the practices of private business. Reformers and political scientists argued that efficiency and economy depended on recognizing the distinction between policy, the preserve of the legislature, and administration, which should be left to the executive.

These are caricatures, but not entirely unfair, as anyone who knew the government reorganization movement of the 1920s and 1930s or read the early textbooks of public administration or read the broadsides of the committee to support the Hoover Report will surely recall. They were echoed, with careful qualifications, by the scholarly types who followed up on the Brownlow report with subsequent plans for reorganization, and they were stated more bluntly by former President Hoover and his staff. Those who recommended the creation and support of the Executive Office felt justified in emphasizing arguments that would strike responsive chords in Congress and the public.

These two lines of argument—business efficiency and the separation of policy from administration—were effective in producing political support, but they probably contributed later on to the distortion of the original principles of the Executive Office in several ways.

The purpose of government reorganizations and of executive staff agencies was defined in terms, not of their true policy objectives, but of eliminating overlapping and duplication and achieving economy.[7] Every reorganization plan was required to make estimates of savings to be effected, a requirement that was usually evaded by one excuse or another but that conditioned the response of members of Congress. The removal of overlapping functions was a purpose that would make sense at the lower hierarchical level of operations and was reasonable in an era in which government functions were few and unimportant. But the impact of modern science and technology and the complexity that they have infused into our economic and social system have made the functions and programs of all major departments interdependent and interlocking; the major purpose of national policy now must be to look to their coherent meshing, not to separate them sharply.

The old Bureau of the Budget (now Office of Management and Budget) was committed by these ideas to tend, in most of its parts, to a negative and restricted outlook. Some of its directors (notably Harold D. Smith, who took it over as it was being moved into the Executive Office) had a broader view of its purpose—to be the President's principal career staff, concerned with policy in the broadest sense and on a nonpartisan basis. It was possible to put together an impressive staff group of this kind in relatively short order because American government officials have never been divided into only the two categories of political and career officers. In the U.S. there is a third category between those two, comprising a great variety of "in-and-outers" who alternate between government service and private employment and are selected less for partisan campaign purposes than for their ability in some program or profession. Some of these "in-and-outers" are highly partisan in their motives, but others, including many who are professionally educated for public policy and administration, come from nonprofit public service institutions and accommodate themselves easily to governmental responsibilities. It was such officers, recruited from universities, state and local governments, and philanthropic institutions, that gave the bureau its reputation for high quality work on broad policy issues.

But it was not easy to maintain such a personnel system in the Executive Office since the pressure of public and congressional expectations worked in the opposite direction and sometimes led the President himself to demand that the bureau help him control a great many detailed decisions that might have been left to his department heads.[8]

The implicit distinction between administration, as something to be left to career officers, and policy, which should be the province of political appointees,[9] may well have discouraged the development of a strong career staff with a good institutional memory, concerned with the more general implications of new policy developments and committed to working on broad issues with the department heads rather than trying to take over managerial control of detailed decisions. Policy issues of importance, it came to be assumed by some later Presidents, had to be dealt with by noncareer staff in order to ensure accountability. This assumption was in sharp contrast not only to the practice of most other democratic governments but also to the practices within the parts of the U.S. government that involve the most critical policy choices—the foreign and military services.

The Brownlow report, as noted in Chapter IV, had proposed that the civil service should occupy positions that were not "policy determining" or "policy forming." These were artful terms. The authors expected civil servants to play important roles in the formulation or development of policy recommendations, while responsibility for ultimate decisions should be made at the political level.[10]

The Hoover Commission reports were less generous to the higher civil service. The first of the two Hoover Commissions almost ig-nored the higher career ranks, and the second commission in 1955, while recommending the creation of a higher civil service of a more generalist nature, tried to draw a sharp line between its public role, to be confined to its managerial responsibilities, and that of its po-litical superiors, with exclusive responsibility for policy advocacy.[11]

It is easy, however, to read back into the documents of a genera-tion ago much more of a clear-cut distinction between policy staff and managerial staff than the facts warrant. The most important staff work for the coordination of legislative policy recommenda-tions was done by the legislative reference division of the Bureau of the Budget, which began to undertake its work in the 1920s at the insistence of congressional committees,[12] and some of the most sig-nificant studies of major policy issues were undertaken by the Di-vision of Administrative Management of the bureau. Such work had been vastly expanded during the Roosevelt presidency. Although the bureau yielded to the President's intimate personal staff on issues of headline importance, it was clear that there was no possibility of drawing a sharp line between the policy and the managerial staff work within the institutional staff agencies of the Executive Office.

The Budget Bureau came very close, for several years, to serving as a generalist staff agency for the President, especially through its staff work on organization and on legislative clearance. It was aided by the fact that its name partially concealed its functions, and its formal statutory role of compiling the budget estimates justified its collection of all sorts of significant policy and program data. Other staff agencies were created, however—the Council of Economic Ad-visers and later the President's Science Advisory Committee—which cut into the bureau's field of influence. Most important, perhaps, the Brownlow Committee idea of reliance on the career civil service for policy staff work began to be eroded. While President Eisen-hower's first budget director, Joseph M. Dodge, had managed to get along with a staff made up entirely of civil service veterans, both his later budget directors and those in President Kennedy's admin-istration began to bring in noncareer assistant and associate direc-tors to head the key policy areas of the bureau.

It was in the sensitive area of personnel that the key principles of the Executive Office reformers were hardest to put into effect. The Brownlow Committee recommendation for abolishing the Civil Service Commission and setting up instead a single-headed administration with a special board to protect the merit system was turned down by Congress, which by statute forbade the President to alter the commission by Reorganization Plan. That reform was not effected until President Carter's Civil Service Reform Act of 1978. And soon thereafter the recurrent political attacks on the career service were reaffirmed in more theoretical terms when in 1980 the new head of the Office of Personnel Management told the American Society for Public Administration that, as career civil servants, they should heed the theories of Max Weber, avoid involvement in policy issues, and confine their efforts to the efficient management of the policies stated by their political superiors.[13]

ABOLISHING STAFF TO FORESTALL POLICY

While the capacity of staff to work at a general policy level has been degraded by assignment to more routine duties, it has also been constrained by a blunter attack. That is the tactic of crippling or abolishing a staff unit in order to prevent the formulation of a policy or program that it may be expected to promote. Those who have been surprised in recent years by what the Reagan administration has done to the Council on Environmental Quality and to the funds and staff for environmental regulation in the Departments of Agriculture, Transportation, and Housing and Urban Development should recall the fate of earlier scientific staff agencies.[14]

In the New Deal years and shortly thereafter, this happened most often when congressional committees that were unhappy with the influence of the social sciences in the direction of expansion of government functions found it more effective, not to debate the substance of the issues, but to abolish the staff work. The most conspicuous example was the National Resources Planning Board (NRPB), the first planning agency included in 1939 in the Executive Office. It exemplified the reliance on the social sciences for the development of new policy: it picked up in various fields the interests of former President Hoover's Committee on Social Trends (a privately supported temporary commission that in later years would have been called a think tank), and it demonstrated how far the Brownlow Committee was from confining its real interests to management in the narrow efficiency sense of that term.

The NRPB had three members, none of them full-time at the job. In terms of substantive policy the most influential was Charles E. Merriam (a member of the Brownlow Committee), who had founded the Social Science Research Council in 1921 and was an influential adviser to the Rockefeller philanthropies. Brownlow himself, though not a formal member, was a regular participant in its deliberations and brought into its orbit the interests of the various associations of public officials (most notably those of the governors, mayors, and city managers), which shared the Chicago headquarters of the Public Administration Clearing House, of which Brownlow was the director.

The NRPB issued public reports on urbanism, science and technology, postwar policy for veterans, and other subjects congenial to New Deal political thought. Its work was done in frequent communication with British officials and scholars, especially with Lord Beveridge, whose report on postwar "cradle to grave" security programs encouraged American liberal politicians, and with Sir Henry Bunbury, whose study of the machinery of governmental planning in various countries encouraged the planning movement in the United States.[15]

All this commitment to social planning, however, was too much for the Congress to take in the early years of World War II, when President Roosevelt had to maintain the support of political conservatives in the interest of the war effort. In 1943 the Planning Board was abolished by the refusal of Congress to appropriate funds for its support, and the institutional agencies in the Executive Office that remained were those with a more strictly administrative perspective.

After World War II, however, the threat of postwar depression led a later Congress to have second thoughts about the issue of planning, and the result was the Employment Act of 1946, which set up the Council of Economic Advisers in the Executive Office. There was no question that it was expected to deal with policy issues, though within an apparently narrower scope, and it never made much pretense of being nonpartisan after its first chairman, Edwin G. Nourse, resigned because his vision of an objective scientific staff avoiding contact with the Congress failed to meet President Truman's needs.[16]

As time went on, the pace of events made it less and less possible for Presidents to deal with their major problems through the agencies embodying the older "tools of management." Science and technology were not only adding to the intricacies of interdepartmental relationships but were also paradoxically both speeding up the pace of developments and making it less possible to deal with issues on short notice. An eighteenth-century militia could be put in the field in a few days or weeks, with every farmer bringing along his own flintlock; a modern nuclear or ballistic missile system takes more than a decade to develop. It was possible for the military services, although they too came under constraints, especially after Vietnam, to develop general and joint staff work and to train members of the career military services as general (which is to say generalist) officers with a view to the long pull. These were not conceivable possibilities for the civilian side of the government, even though civilian agencies, faced by problems like medical care, technological innovation, urban development, or energy, had problems of equal complexity and demanding an equally long-range capacity for foresight and sustained policy.

Instead of relying on career staff officers in some of these complex fields, successive Presidents tried to develop special arrangements to recruit scientific advisers from nongovernmental sources. The President's Science Advisory Committee, chaired by the President's Special Assistant for Science and Technology and supported by numerous panels including scientists from private institutions, was set up under President Eisenhower. That was the high point of the involvement of American scientists in public affairs. But the effort to give the scientific establishment direct access to the peak of political authority had its problems, especially when the advisers were called on to deal with civilian issues unprotected from public or congressional scrutiny by military secrecy.

In 1973 President Nixon, shortly after a member of the President's Science Advisory Committee testified before a congressional committee in opposition to one of the President's projects, the supersonic transport, abolished the committee altogether. The President's petulance was reminiscent, in a very mild way, of King Henry's appeal to his retainers about Thomas à Becket—"who will rid me of this troublesome priest?" But the martyrdom of Saint Thomas had no counterpart in modern Washington: the offending scientists retreated to the universities and the National Academy and continued their conflicts with the political leadership. It is clear, however, that the more the science advisers rely, as their tradition of dissent tempts them to do, on the evidence of their discipline and the less they like to suppress their scruples and compromise with the career officials concerned with the same issues, the more they find it difficult to fit into the executive hierarchy.[17]

Later Presidents never restored the scientific advisers to quite their former status. One may only speculate about the reasons. But it seems likely that the leadership of the scientific community, as organized in the National Academy of Sciences and its affiliates, remained rather more liberal in its outlook on international and military problems and, indeed, on some environmental and health regulatory programs than suited the taste of President Nixon and most of his successors during the 1970s. Later Presidents tried to deal with the problem, especially in view of the congressional committees with which they had to negotiate, by bringing to the Executive Office as advisers fewer academic scientists and more engineers from industry, but even such measures failed to bring harmony into the relationship. In any case, it had not seemed possible to set up within the Executive Office a scientific advisory staff of adequate quality on a career basis, and part-time or short-term advisers were too much committed to their own independent policy views and too unwilling to remain anonymous in public discussion of these views, to let them fit comfortably into the President's staff system.

PREFERENCE FOR ADVICE FROM PRIVATE INSTITUTIONS

Political staff work is one thing, and the provision of staff advice based on scientific competence is another. The political staffer depends for influence on proximity to the President; the scientific adviser is more likely to be comfortable in his role if he operates from an independent base in a private institution, and his advice from such a base is likely to have greater political weight.

The leading scientific advisers for Presidents Eisenhower and Kennedy were chosen and did their work with little regard to partisan politics. They were sustained in that approach by their memories of service in the research and development programs of World War II, when political differences were submerged by patriotism. But that sense of dedication began to wane as scientists began to be more skeptical of the military leadership, and vice versa, and as the subjects under consideration began to involve domestic policy issues, on which there was more partisan controversy.

Accordingly, some of the leading scientists began to pull out of service in the President's staff and to try to build up on a modern basis the independent capability of the National Academy of Sciences as adviser to the government. The creation in 1962 of the Committee on Science and Public Policy of the academy and the later establishment of the National Academy of Engineering and the Institute of Medicine as its affiliates were steps in the process of providing a base for independent study and public advice by scientists on much the same kinds of topics as had engaged the attention of the President's Science Advisory Committee. As noted above (Chapter IV) Congress responded, welcoming the opportunity to call on such talent as a counterbalance to presidential influence, and required various agencies to support a series of major studies by the academy with generous contracts.

The academy, while controlled by its members who remain private citizens, is nevertheless a public, or at least quasi-public institution, set up by act of Congress and listed in the U.S. Government Manual. Its advisory influence, however, is probably less than that of the multitude of privately incorporated research firms and consulting institutions, some of them set up at federal initiative and supported heavily by federal money, commonly called the think tanks. The most influential of these has probably been the Rand Corporation, organized to serve the air force by scientific and strategic studies. Its prestige was so great as to suggest that the competition among the military services for roles and missions might be reduced if the underlying strategic and technical issues were studied by an independent institution, controlled and supported by a board of eminent private trustees.

The idea appealed in 1953 to the Committee on the Organization of the Department of Defense, chaired by Nelson A. Rockefeller, which was trying to carry forward for President Eisenhower the efforts of the first Hoover Commission to strengthen presidential control over the military. It recommended that the Weapons Systems Evaluation Group, a research agency for the Joint Chiefs of Staff that had relied mainly on career officials, be provided with an operations research staff by the contract method.[18] Accordingly, a new private corporation, the Institute for Defense Analyses, was created by a consortium of leading universities, and took over the work in 1956. But it found within a few years that scientific expertise was no substitute for political authority: the competing strategic views of the military services could not be integrated by research reports. The institute lost its role in this effort after Robert McNamara became secretary of defense in 1961 and put his own staff (several of them Rand alumni) to work on the analytic problems that could not be handled by an institution that had to depend on the consensus of competing services; the WSEG itself was finally abolished in 1976.

The Rand Corporation itself had similar difficulties as it tried to serve not only the air force, but also the secretary of defense or the Executive Office of the President. If a single military service deserves high quality research support, why should not the President or, for that matter, the Congress? Both doubtless should. The question ought instead to be why are they unlikely to pay for such support from a single private corporation?

One aspect of the answer is theoretical. The hierarchical structure of policy-making is, from the point of view of pure science, upside-down. Science is reductionist, most powerful when it deals with questions that (from the point of view of the politician) are abstract and specialized or that deal more with technical than with policy issues. The higher echelons of government are likely to leave to subordinates all those questions that science can clearly answer; at the top the politician must struggle with issues that cut across scientific specialties. He can get tremendous help from science, but only if he first defines the question that he wants it to answer. The choice of the question normally reflects the policy and the purposes of the officer who asks it.

The other reason the government is unlikely to rely for its scientific advice on a single private corporation is tactical. Science is unpredictable. If scientists are licensed to work on questions of their own choice that go beyond technical issues and involve broader questions of policy (as any analysis of a systematic nature must do), their results may well not be acceptable to public officials who are responsible for carrying out a set policy. The Rand Corporation got more freedom to do research on issues of its own choice than other think tanks as a result of the unusual circumstances of its foundation: it had a substantial private endowment; it was located on the west coast, well away from Washington; and it served the newest of the three armed services, which had become accustomed to contracting out to private corporations many functions that in the older services were tightly held by career officers. Yet it ran into trouble when its staff tried to do work for higher echelons. Impartial studies for those levels in the hierarchy were all too likely to support conclusions that might damage the competitive position of Rand's main client, the air force, as against the army or navy.[19]

Military secrecy can keep studies of particular weapons systems out of the newspapers, but research for higher levels of authority is harder to keep secret and more likely to have political impact. For similar reasons, a President is unlikely to put his political fortunes at the mercy of scientists who are politically unreliable, and an appropriations committee in Congress is unlikely to provide funds for a research institution that might feel obliged to produce reports either in support of a President's partisan interests or against them in favor of some faction in Congress.[20]

The kinds of scientific research and analytic studies that could be of use to a President are accordingly hard to organize on a regular basis within the Executive Office. It is somewhat easier to establish them within subordinate units in the departments, easier still in quasi-governmental institutions like the National Academy or the federal contract research centers, and—if money is available—still easier to set them up as private institutions or associations. The research that provided the intellectual stimulation for the New Deal was done by academic-type research programs supported by philanthropic foundations; by the 1980s, although the foundations were still active, the more conservative influence was being exercised by a great variety of private institutions supported by businessmen interested in direct political action. Thus the California group that undertook to back the political career of Ronald Reagan founded the Institute for Contemporary Studies,[21] and the Heritage Foundation came to be considered in some circles the arbiter of properly conservative policy. At least some members of Congress thought so: forty-three of them, believing that President Reagan was deserting the conservative principles he had articulated in his 1980 campaign, urged him to take guidance on his political appointments from the Heritage Foundation.[22]

As long as elected legislators find it more effective to control policy outcomes, not by legislation dealing with policy issues, but by manipulating the organization and management processes within the executive, a President is forced (or at least tempted) to bargain away his long-run interest in building up a generalist staff, in order to gain short-run political ends. The Executive Office staff agencies have never been left to the President's discretionary control so that he could develop his capacity to propose coherent long-range policies for decision by the Congress.

The Cabinet and Committees

These failures to develop the staff work in the Executive Office on its original principles made more difficult the second aspect of its purpose: the effective consultation on policy issues with cabinet members. The recurrent idea that the President should not control policy mainly through his staff, but should rely instead on "cabinet government," has been derided by cynical observers of White House politics. But it would be a mistake, while emphasizing the difficulties that cabinet-level committees have encountered, to ignore the contribution that has been made to the coordination of policy by efforts to organize these committees properly.

The use of such committees was no new idea at the time the Executive Office was established in 1939. President Roosevelt had tried to pull the New Deal into a more orderly system by his creation not only of various coordinating committees in special fields, such as the Central Housing Committee, but also of a comprehensive committee, the National Emergency Council, including both cabinet members and the heads of emergency agencies. The council had as its executive director Frank C. Walker, formerly chairman of the Democratic National Committee and later postmaster general. It was abolished and its functions were transferred by Reorganization Plan to the new Executive Office of the President when that office was created in 1939.

During the Second World War, President Roosevelt's firm grip on the organization of the war agencies made irrelevant any idea of a more formal set of cabinet procedures. But after the war, and with a new and inexperienced President in office, a lively debate developed over the possible ways in which more efficient interdepartmental collaboration could be organized and managed.

A clear split developed between two schools of thought. On one side were those who wanted a formal system established by law, by which department heads and their top assistants could have a voice in executive policies, and on the other side were those who feared that any such formal system would restrict the flexibility of presidential policy and management and encourage encroachment by congressional committees. Both sides of the argument were directly influenced by their study of British experience with the Cabinet committees and secretariat. The side that preferred a formal system attracted far more public attention and may be noted first, even though it came later in time.

During the Second World War the necessity of collaborating with the British led first to the creation of the Combined Chiefs of Staff, U.S. and U.K. Within this organization the American participants found themselves divided and uninformed in comparison with their British counterparts; the result was that they were obliged to ask the President to authorize the establishment of the U.S. Joint Chiefs of Staff, which was only later sanctioned by act of Congress.

Several years later, after he became secretary of state, General Marshall recalled how often he and his fellow chiefs, needing to know the outcome of FDR's meetings with Churchill, had to go to the British Joint Staff Mission in the Pentagon to find out what decisions had been made by their own commander in chief.[23] This humiliating experience led to studies by the U.S. Joint Chiefs of Staff of the British Cabinet secretariat and its procedures and to a staff paper proposing that the United States should consider creating a similar system to integrate military and civilian policy.[24] The paper was in effect suppressed since Admiral Leahy, as chairman of the Joint Chiefs of Staff while serving as FDR's personal adviser, considered it improper for the military to propose civilian constitutional arrangements. But General Marshall educated Secretary Forrestal, the first head of the semi-unified National Military Establishment, in these matters after the war, and Secretary Forrestal, a complete convert, began to distribute all over Washington copies of the book by Lord Hankey which explained the history and procedures of the Cabinet committee and secretariat system that had been developed under his direction.[25] During the Truman administration the possibility of creating something like a cabinet secretariat and committee system for the United States was one of the hottest topics of conversation in bureaucratic and political circles.

The issue was not whether the government needed a system for the management of interdepartmental policy discussions and joint program planning. It was clear that it did. Nor was it an issue whether the traditional managerial staff agencies were adequate for the job. They clearly were not. The key issue was of course the question of presidential discretion in the direction of interdepartmental relations, as against a formalized or statutory system that would give groups of department heads more of an opportunity, by consensus or vote, to put forward policy advice that would gather congressional support (or respond to congressional pressure) and that the President would find it hard to reject.

As early as the First World War, there had been lively controversy in Congress over the proposal to create something like a council of national defense, which was to be set up by statute with more or less actual authority over decisions and more or less responsibility for advising the President.[26] Wilson had defeated a move to put what he regarded as his essential responsibilities under the control of a statutory council. Much the same issue had arisen in the 1930s with the argument over the M-Day plan—the Industrial Mobilization Plan of 1939.[27] Working with Brownlow's advice, Roosevelt had forestalled the granting of statutory authority over war mobilization to anything like a council on national defense, and through the Office for Emergency Management that had been created in the new Executive Office, he retained discretionary control over the pattern of organization.

Not many people in Washington expected that a similar degree of presidential control could be exercised by FDR's successor—and especially not the members of the cabinet that Truman inherited. Some of them felt uneasy about serving under a President with no federal executive experience, who as vice-president had not even been informed about many of the secret arrangements for the conduct of the war, including the development of the atomic bomb.[28]

This atmosphere of distrust of the new President's leadership, within the Executive Branch as well as in the Congress, persisted from the end of the war in 1945 to the election of 1948 when Truman surprised almost everyone, including many of his intimate subordinates, by winning over Dewey. During this period, the pressure for a more formalized system of cabinet committees intensified. If it seemed impossible to establish the kind of secretariat for the whole cabinet that the Joint Chiefs of Staff had suggested—and General Marshall's hope for such a secretariat waned when his candidate for the secretary's job, Averell Harriman, was made ambassador to the Soviet Union in 1943—[29] perhaps something could be done on a more limited basis for the coordination of military and international affairs.

Those who were most strongly in favor of this idea were the military leaders who wanted to be sure that civilian politicians would not make major national commitments on national security problems without their advice. Among the military departments and their civilian heads, the navy was especially eager to maintain an independent political position and to avoid being submerged by President Truman's proposal for unification of the armed services. As a strategy for this purpose, Secretary of the Navy Forrestal led the campaign with congressional leaders to enact a statutory pattern of interagency consultation. The result was the National Security Act of 1947 creating a weak National Military Establishment, a strong

Joint Chiefs of Staff, and a National Security Council and National Security Resources Board, both outside the Executive Office of the President but with major responsibilities for the planning of international and military policy.

The National Security Council was in effect to replace the cabinet as the President's advisory body on national security affairs, but originally its members included only one secretary of a nonmilitary department, the secretary of state, who was overbalanced by the several secretaries of the military departments and the members of the Joint Chiefs. The intent of the legislation was to have the President, after chairing the discussion of the issues with the members of the council, make his decisions forthwith. Truman, however, refused to be put on the spot in such a way. He appointed an old Kansas City friend, General Sidney Souers, as secretary of the council; decided that as President he would not normally attend its meetings; instructed Souers to have the recommendations of the council reported to him; but insisted on having decisions on the issues communicated as presidential directives, not as decisions of the council—a procedure in effect ever since.[30]

For the longer run, however, the degree of authority to be given statutory cabinet councils was restricted by the persistent efforts of the Brownlow allies and their successors, and of the first Hoover Commission. Their Constitutional view was that the President should be no more obliged to consult groups of subordinates defined by statute or give particular weight to their advice than he was obliged to do with respect to the cabinet itself. The cabinet, of course, was never established or defined by statute, and its recommendations were not made public in ways that the President might find it awkward to reject.

The Brownlow Committee had not failed to consider the British Cabinet system as a possible model, nor had it been uninterested in Executive Office arrangements for dealing with policy issues. The participation of its members in the work of the National Resources Planning Board and their sustained interest in planning and policy development at the municipal and state level had proved their concern. Indeed, as a city manager in the early 1920s Brownlow had held out stoutly against the academic theorists who had argued that city managers should be neutral in policy and concerned only with economy and efficiency of management; his view was that a manager's main duty was one of policy leadership on a nonpartisan basis.

As for the British Cabinet model, the Brownlow Committee had commissioned a study of it by William Y. Elliott, professor of government at Harvard and an avowed admirer of the parliamentary system. Elliott's formula for American Constitutional reform, it should be noted, would have given the President the right to dissolve a refractory Congress, but not the Congress the right to dismiss the President.[31] His research paper, however, recommended something like a cabinet system and secretariat for the President; the committee rejected it as a guide to its report and did not have it published among its supporting documents in 1937.

During World War II, Brownlow himself became obsessed with the necessity for a more effective system of interdepartmental policy development to balance the managerial staff work in the Executive Office. He prepared a paper on the subject, which the members of the National Resources Planning Board transmitted personally and confidentially to President Roosevelt in 1943.[32] In this paper he went far beyond the notions of "tools of management" in the staff agencies of the Executive Office and recommended a network of cabinet committees, each covering a major field of public policy and chaired by an agent of the President and all operated through a secretariat of career staff members. The President rejected the idea and the paper remained buried in the archives for a quarter century.[33]

Similarly, after the discussions of cabinet committees and secretariats during the first Truman administration, Herbert Hoover and his first Commission on Organization (at the insistence of one of its members, Secretary Forrestal, by that time head of the National Military Establishment) confronted directly the issues of the use of cabinet committees and the need for a cabinet secretariat. They agreed with Secretary Forrestal on the need for more systematic consultation of cabinet members in appropriate groups. But their final collective decision was to reject the term "cabinet secretariat." Mr. Hoover, referring back to his experience with European governments, disliked the term *secretariat*. The commission went only so far as to propose that the President be authorized to appoint a "staff secretary" and to use him to guide the deliberations of his department heads in a flexible and responsible way. For this purpose, it came out flatly against statutory prescriptions for cabinet committees; instead, it recommended that the President be given full discretionary freedom unhampered by statutory constraints with respect to the creation of cabinet committees and the selection of their membership and their agendas. Perhaps more important in practice, it recommended specifically that the National Security Council and National Security Resources Board be transferred into the Executive Office of the President.[34]

President Truman, supported by the advice of the Bureau of the Budget and its administrative management staff (many of them Brownlow disciples and trainees) had already taken procedural steps to make it clear that the NSC was not to make decisions, and not to take up any agenda item except on his instructions. Now, with the Hoover Commission's blessing, he moved the NSC and NSRB into the Executive Office by a Reorganization Plan. The main issue was settled: like the President's cabinet itself, the NSC was to be an advisory group for the President to use or ignore at his discretion.

This arrangement continued under President Eisenhower, whose military experience had made him more willing to delegate to his department heads than most Presidents and, at the same time, more inclined to do so through a formal system of committee consultation. During his administration, he put more emphasis on regularizing the procedures in his cabinet and in the Operations Coordinating Board under the NSC. He also toyed with the idea that something should be done to relieve the President of the exceptional strain imposed on him by his dual role as chief of state and head of government, a double burden that he found particularly difficult at times of international conferences. He consulted off and on with his President's Advisory Committee on Government Organization about the possibility of creating a First Secretary of the Government, who could serve under the President as the equivalent of other countries' prime ministers. But he never gave the notion high enough priority to recommend it publicly.[35]

On the main issue of giving statutory status to the cabinet or a cabinet committee with broad scope, the Hoover Commission formula has apparently been decisive. But in various specific fields since then Congress has tried to push particular programs by setting up statutory committees within the Executive Office. The most notable effort was during the Eisenhower administration, when Senator Lyndon B. Johnson put through a statute creating the National Aeronautics and Space Council. His purpose was of course to force the President to give more backing to the space program especially in view of the early Soviet successes in that field. President Eisenhower's response was to neglect to appoint a secretary of the new council and to keep it from meeting often enough to have any influence. When Senator Johnson became Vice-President Johnson, President Kennedy gave him the nominal leadership over the space program. He brought in as secretary of the new council a staff member from the Senate, who the Senate Space Committee thought would give its members a measure of control over this new piece of the Executive Office. They were disappointed, and after Johnson became President very little was heard of the Space Council.

Similarly, those members of Congress who wished to give special emphasis to environmental problems pressed the President to set up a cabinet council in that field. Before it had much chance to make a name for itself, or to give its congressional backers any influential pipelines into the Executive Office, President Nixon by a Reorganization Plan and executive action merged it into his new Domestic Council, which was to be the counterpart for domestic affairs of the National Security Council. Under its broad umbrella, the specialized program interests, including urban and rural as well as environmental affairs, were lost to view.[36]

Nixon used, however, an even more effective tactic for preventing a special congressional interest from controlling a part of his office, and this tactic he inherited from President Kennedy. Kennedy had not admired Eisenhower's systematic reliance on committees, and instead of meeting frequently with the National Security Council, he paid it little attention and used the staff that was formally attached to it as his own, making McGeorge Bundy his special assistant for national security affairs. President Nixon, in a similar way, relied on Henry Kissinger in that staff job, and when the Domestic Council was set up, used John Ehrlichman in a similar way.

Presidents have learned, it seems, not to be trapped into dealing with statutory committees in ways that will restrict their discretion in getting advice in the ways that best suit their political convenience. But cabinet committees or councils, if they can be set up in ways that are not restrictive, may still be found useful by Presidents. President Ford's Economic Policy Board set a pattern that President Reagan has imitated in some of his cabinet councils. Under a central White House secretariat, the President has a series of committees at the cabinet level, each set up by informal order, subject to change at the President's pleasure, and served by secretaries on the Executive Office staff. As long as these councils are left entirely to presidential discretion, they may do much to balance the staff agencies in providing help for the President.[37] And if the President requires (or permits) them to operate on a confidential basis, avoiding the temptation to exploit their proceedings for short-term legislative advantage, they may make use of a mix of career staff and "in-and-outers" in ways that support the responsibilities of the secretaries of departments and encourage a broader view of long-range policy issues.

The Confusion of Principles

The Executive Office of the President could not be made to conform to its original principles not because they were wrong but because they were undermined by the basic attitudes of the reform groups on which they relied for support. Those ideas, in caricature, were the beliefs in scientism, or the settlement of policy issues by expertise; legalism, or the delegation of administrative authority by formal law; and reformism, or the weakening of responsible authority by the destruction of party discipline.

As for scientism, the presidency is confronted by a career public service that was largely rescued from patronage by the imposition of scientific and professional standards, with the result that the several functional specialties were improved in their administration but became more resistant to coordination from the Executive Office. That office itself, by the creation of specialized staff units like the National Security Council, the Council of Economic Advisers, the Council on Environmental Quality, and the Office of Science and

Technology Policy, was a victim of the same overrated reliance on expertise—the various types of expertise that are absolutely necessary to any modern government but must be balanced against each other and controlled by general policy. The incentive system that produces presidential advisers from scientific or specialized fields subordinates the career officer to the specialist who has made his reputation in private institutions and will serve only for short periods, retaining his connections with colleagues and potential employers in private life.

As for legalism, the original debate over the reorganization plan creating the Executive Office was over the Constitution's provisions regarding the control of the departments and agencies. The theory of the Brownlow Committee, as it came to be argued in vulgar form, was that under the Constitution the President was the head of the executive branch and that Congress should not interfere with his management of it. The opposing view was that of Lewis Meriam and his colleagues at the Brookings Institution, which was working with the Senate committee on reorganization chaired by Senator Harry Byrd. They held that the departments and agencies constituted an administrative branch set up by acts of Congress and were therefore under the Congress rather than the President.

The Brookings argument went back to the views of W. F. Willoughby, who as early as 1921 was arguing that the administrative branch was under the Congress rather than the President but who was then using that theory to advocate that the President's executive office should enable him, with congressional support, to become the general manager of the government as a whole.[38]

Since the Constitution does not mention branches of government at all and, by its distribution of powers, thoroughly confuses the presumed separation of powers, it might be just as well to acknowledge that as a descriptive (though not as a normative) matter the old Brookings interpretation had much merit. Through its committees, Congress had long since taken over a major part of the control of administration: its legislation determined the missions of executive departments and the pattern of organization and personnel systems, its appropriations systems controlled the details of expenditure, and its agent, the General Accounting Office, settled all accounts.

On the other hand, such administrative authority as the President had (or now has) is the result of action taken by the Congress to delegate to him, especially through its enactment of the civil service system, the budget system, and other procedures for planning and management. If the President has control over administrative matters it is not the result of the written Constitution but of delegation from the Congress, either by enacting explicit statutes or by refraining from interference. As we have already noted, even if such delegation is granted by explicit statutory enactment, it may be withdrawn by informal political pressure, as was shown by the constraints on the Hoover Commission's reforms giving department heads legal authority over their subordinate bureau chiefs. The Brownlow Committee appeal to the President's Constitutional position may have been useful as a pious appeal to tradition, but it did not have enduring effect in persuading Congress to delegate authority.

It may be worth reiterating that the sales pitches by which the Brownlow and the Hoover reports were promoted were not accurate reflections of the total insights or intentions of the authors of those reports. They were compromises, conditioned by the fact that the reports had to be presented to Congress and had to stay within the limits of the ideas that were conventionally acceptable and politically feasible. Even more important, the efforts to translate the reports into action were distorted by the fact that they depended on changes in congressional organization and procedures which the interested members of the President's staff were inhibited from advocating. The Brownlow report had proposed that Congress set up special or joint committees to oversee the work of each of the President's managerial staff agencies (budgeting, personnel, and planning), but this recommendation was ignored by Congress and promptly forgotten by scholars.[39]

As for reformism, the original political supporters of the Executive Office included many who were opposed not only to political patronage but also to party discipline. Their faith was in political pluralism, rational deliberation, and independent or nonpartisan voting both by the electorate and by members of Congress, as opposed to the domination of particular party doctrine, ideology, or political log-rolling. This attitude was in harmony with faith in scientism and legalism, and the combination of the three made it hard to emphasize political accountability as a primary objective of the institutional presidency.

Political accountability is not enforced by an audit of literal compliance with specific statutes but rather by the need to muster political support for the kind of discretionary authority required to deal with conflicting values and the determination of general political goals. Science cannot determine those goals or values but can only help answer the question how best to reach goals determined by political leadership. And as for nonpartisan reform, the maximum accountability of the executive to the Congress would not be accomplished by breaking the executive agencies up into 535 pieces and giving one to each member of Congress to administer; the problem is rather how to get a greater degree of coherence and integration in the total pattern by some kind of political organization and discipline.

The complexities of policy in a scientific age were calling for guiding hypotheses of a comprehensive and unifying nature—hypotheses or, if you prefer, a political value system—within which rational and scientific staff members might find the questions that they would be expected to answer. The central leadership to pose such questions and give the necessary guidance could not be established without the kind of party cohesion which political reformers were undertaking to break down.

For a brief time after the Brownlow and Hoover reports, the President still had strong political leadership within the Congress with which to bargain and from which to get a reasonable degree of political support. Speaker Byrns, Speaker Rayburn, and Senator Vandenberg all exemplified the power to bargain with Presidents and deliver on their bargains. But the attitudes of scientism, legalism, and reformism on which the institutional presidency relied for support continued to handicap it in the management of policy.

The old formulas have become inadequate for thinking about the institutional presidency. The President's institutional system for defining a coherent policy is not established or protected by the Constitution. It is not adequately described as the management of the government's business. And as an argument to persuade Congress to delegate adequately to the President, the distinction between policy and administration is useless: the most important step in the formulation of a policy is the development of an institutional system and procedures to work on the subject—a process that is highly vulnerable to political sabotage.

The crucial difficulty with both policy and administration in American government is that party discipline would be no help in dealing with major issues of national policy as long as members of Congress have little incentive to concern themselves with such issues but powerful incentives to concentrate on the "oversight"—a euphemism for administrative direction—of fragments of programs. Worse still, they are tempted to control those programs not by formal statutes, which would require action of the Congress as a whole, but by informal collusion with subordinate bureaucrats, which transfers effective power to the subcommittees or their staffs. They are also tempted not to oppose policies in public debate but to cripple them by impeding their administration. And so, of course, is the President.

A more effective approach would have to command a consensus between the major political parties; it would amount to an agreement on how the unwritten constitution of the United States should operate. It might well, in matters of administration, put primary emphasis not on efficiency but on accountability and, in politics, less on legalism and more on responsibility. We may well ask what that would involve, in view of our traditional commitment to ideas derived from the old religious dissenters and the new scientists.

VI

Accountability Under the Unwritten Constitution

The vision of a society made perfect by the control of an ideological elite may still support autocracy in some parts of the world, but it is hardly the most dangerous dream of the United States. The greater American temptation is at the other extreme. From colonial days, Americans have sought to escape even responsible authority by various automatic formulas for salvation or for secular perfectibility. It began with the confidence that depraved humanity would reach the millennium by the grace of God, and since then at various times various elites—eager to escape the burdens of political responsibility—have put their faith in endless technological progress or the free market or some even less plausible dogma. But the contemporary world is complex enough and dangerous enough so that even those who disapprove of politics and distrust government on principle must grope for some system of disciplined organization. In a polity that has always distrusted establishments, how may such a system be held responsible through representative democratic processes?

The Western European and, especially, the British answer to the same question has been—after various revolutionary experiments—to entrust the job of governing to the old establishment but to put it under the control of a cabinet responsible to an elected legislature. This meant that the electorate's major line of control—

especially in Great Britain—was exercised by a single big check: to vote a majority party out of office.

The American approach was to start with nearly a clean slate: the bureaucratic establishment was minimal, with no corporate continuity or power, and the agencies of political power had continually to be created anew, with fresh delegation of authority, in order to function. But that delegation was jealously restricted by the attitudes derived from the early doctrines of the religious dissenters and reenforced by the new influence of the scientists. The electorate's control over American government accordingly became diffuse and incoherent, with multiple checks through legislative committees and specialized executive bureaus, subject to little unity of political doctrine.

After the divine right of kings lost out to the voice of the people as the ultimate basis of political power, it became necessary to work out some new way to translate that power into practice, with proper responsibility. In administrative operation *vox populi* sometimes seems as hard to identify as *vox dei*. Politicians and their general administrators have to obey the democratic decisions of the electorate and then translate them into action with the help of various types of professional experts—the lawyers, whose systematic knowledge was based on philosophy derived originally from theology, and the scientific professionals in fields like medicine, engineering, economics, or agriculture.

May we reasonably expect such a process to further the public interest in any consistent way? Political theorists argue whether there is really any such thing as the public interest or whether that is only a name for the hodgepodge of special interests that are claimants on tax dollars. That recalls the arguments between the realists and the nominalists of the Middle Ages. The nominalist view—that the "public interest" is only a name without any real content—is made plausible by the way the American government operates today. Those who make an earnest effort to make the public interest a reality have to work out some notion as to how the will of millions of voters, expressed through polls or elections, may exercise some coherent control over the diverse functions of government. Such control will depend in part on the constitutional arrangements but then also on the ways in which science and religion contribute to the development of public policies.

Delegation by the Electorate and by Congress

The electorate may exercise control only if it delegates extensively to the Congress and the President and then permits them to delegate to the operating agencies in some hierarchical pattern. It is hard for the voters to accept this necessity: they may understand that a business executive is subject to an iron law of delegation and that the surest way for him to lose control is to try to make too many decisions himself. But the average citizen wants his member of Congress to intervene in decisions that affect his special or local interest and indignantly agrees when a television reporter criticizes the President for not jumping in with an instant decision on any special issue that hits the headlines.

The most irresponsible political executives are those who try to make all the detailed decisions for which they might be held responsible. Franklin Roosevelt and Ronald Reagan have been among those Presidents who refused to make that mistake. In government as well as in business, the effective leader is the one who is willing to delegate—to concentrate on the big and the long-range issues and to leave the immediate petty problems to subordinates.

This approach breaks down, however, if a leader's subordinates are disloyal to him or under the control of someone else. In American government, this breakdown comes about because we Americans do not realize that the iron law of delegation applies not only to the executives but also to the Congress from which they get their power and to which they are vulnerable as well as accountable. Even more important, it also applies to us as voters—the parties and pressure groups and the media of communications by which they are swayed. Any level of authority can be wrecked by an overload of specific duties or fragmented if delegation from above bypasses it and goes directly to subordinates. If the voters (and their political leaders) do not realize that they cannot directly control the details of government but must delegate to accountable institutions, they overload the system, and the result is less rather than more democratic control. American experience proved this as the "long ballot" (the election of minor administrative officers in the states and cities) led in the nineteenth century to boss rule rather than responsible government and as an exaggerated reliance on direct democracy through the initiative and referendum has weakened the accountability of legislatures.

The next level of delegation, from the Congress to those to whom it delegates various types of power, is a crucial one in the system of accountability. It is tempting to note the obvious conflict between Capitol Hill and the White House and to consider that conflict the key to the difficulties in American government. That view makes plausible the proposition that the separation of powers is the source of the incoherence and inconsistency of American policies and that a constitutional reform is needed to imitate the parliamentary cabinet system.

The conflict between Congress and the President, however, is not as difficult a problem as another conflict—especially difficult because it is not so obvious. That is the conflict between Congress and itself—between Congress as a whole and its own committees and staffs. It is not obvious or apparent because Congress prefers, as an organized and disciplined entity, not to exist. It rather prefers to leave its undisciplined parts in control of pieces of its business. This process is not one of real delegation, because delegation implies accountability, and there is no effective way to hold the committees or staffs fully and publicly accountable to the whole Congress. And it prevents the Congress from delegating in the Constitutional way— to the President and the legally accountable heads of departments and agencies—by assigning them specific statutory powers and granting them funds and then letting them use those powers and funds with an adequate degree of discretion. The inability of Congress to control its own parts leads many of its members to wish that they did not have the power to make difficult policy decisions—a wish that takes its most striking form in the support for a Constitutional amendment to require a balanced budget.

It is this conflict between Congress and its own parts that would make it futile, for the purpose of settling the problems between the Congress and the President, to amend the Constitution to abolish the so-called separation of powers. The purpose of such a change, in structural terms, would be to give the legislature and the executive mutual control over each other's tenure, as a prime minister may dissolve a legislature that refused to support his policies and as a legislature may vote no confidence in a prime minister and thus force him out of office. In either case, both sides of the struggle appeal to the voters for a final decision.

Essentials of Parliamentary System

The act of demanding a vote of confidence in the House of Commons on a crucial issue is a dramatic and impressive ritual, but its drama obscures the essence of the British parliamentary system. (To what extent that system has been eroded over the past decade is a matter of some controversy, which we need not settle here.) What has made that system work in the United Kingdom, unlike some of those democracies that have imitated the system and bungled it, is what precedes and follows the dramatic act. For the appeal to the electorate makes sense only if it is on an issue clear enough and important enough for the voters to understand—whether the issue be one of substantive policy or the choice between two or three coherent and disciplined parties—so that their verdict can then make a significant difference.

The essence of the British system has been that the prime minister has two basic powers: first he is able, without legislative interference, to define the crucial problem and propose its solution, and second, he can then be confident that if he wins the vote (either in the Commons or in a new election) he will have full authority to accomplish his ends without niggling legislative checks on the required means, such as his selection of those to do the jobs required and the definition of their several responsibilities. It is these powers that have made the parliamentary system work in a democratic way in the United Kingdom and other parts of the old commonwealth. The lack of them has confused the system in certain other democracies, most notably the Third French Republic and the Weimar Republic. It is enough to justify the old observation of Bolingbroke, which Edmund Burke quoted with approval, that it is harder to graft a monarchy onto a republic, than a republic onto a monarchy.[1]

The British have grafted on some of the features of a republic, but the government remains a monarchy. Unlike the confused mixture of powers and functions shared by the American President and Congress, the British have an effective separation of functions that is guaranteed by their formal unification of power, not in the legislature, but in the King (or Queen) in Parliament. This distinction involves the historic tradition of the ministers' loyalty to the Crown, their indoctrination through long service in the Commons, their lifetime membership in the Privy Council, their jealous protection of the rights of the Crown in preventing the Commons from establishing any committees that could rival the responsibility of the Privy Council and the Cabinet, and most important, their complex relationship of mutual support with the establishment that is the successor of the established church as the institutional prop of the monarchy—His Majesty's Civil Service.

The British system does not protect the executive against the legislature by legally enforceable guarantees. The Parliament may, if it chooses, destroy any of the essentials of the system, but it has—so far—accepted them as fundamental: it has no legislative committees that can force major policy changes that the Cabinet disapproves; it cannot even consider any appropriation that has not been requested by the Prime Minister; and its committees, like the ministers themselves, are expected to rely mainly on such staff assistance as the career head of the civil service may assign them.

The American system, on the other hand, could not, by any imaginable provisions in a written constitution, protect a chief executive against legislative encroachment if it made his tenure dependent on a vote in Congress. As we have noted, the main types of interference are not by formal enactment but by political bargains in the process of deliberations on administrative details—by "legislative history" rather than by statutes. Even now, a President must, before putting a legislative program together, bargain with members of Congress to make sure he is within striking distance of getting majority support. If his tenure were at stake on every decision, including decisions on the appointment of his principal subordinates, his position would be hopeless; he would find the top career officers in every department, as well as his cabinet members, bargaining against his policy with committees of Congress and their staffs—even more than they do now.

Even with fixed tenure, we have had trouble learning in the United States that Constitutional provisions cannot guarantee a strong executive. There is no doubt that the framers of the Constitution wished to give the President a measure of independence as the head of administration, as Madison and Hamilton argued in the *Federalist Papers* (especially Nos. 48, 70, 71, and 72). They obviously preferred not to follow the example of the majority of the original thirteen states in which the governors were elected by the legislatures. But our mid-nineteenth-century history justified John Adams' gloomy prediction (as noted in Chapter IV) that Congress would usurp the President's proper role in administration. And it is by no means clear that the United States has yet achieved the right balance in the accountability of the presidency to the Congress.

The lesson that the United States might well learn from the United Kingdom, however, is not to imitate the parliamentary system by formal amendment of the Constitution but to imitate its essence—at least to some extent—by changes in our unwritten constitution. It is hard to imagine Congress deciding by informal political agreement to subject the executive to only a single big test of accountability, such as a parliamentary vote of no confidence, rather than the multitude of little checks that now destroy the coherence of national policy. But it is even harder to imagine that it would permit an amendment to the written Constitution that would make such a change.

THE NEED FOR DELEGATION

But it is possible to imagine—and we may well consider—how Congress might move to insure a somewhat higher degree of executive accountability by changes in the unwritten constitution and then ask how far in that direction it ought to go.

As for how Congress might do so, it would only need to continue the process by which, for nearly a century, it has delegated to the President the measure of administrative authority that he now enjoys. If it does so, it should surely take steps to strengthen substantially its ability, as a whole, to hold him accountable.

The first step in the right direction would be to quit talking about the Constitutional separation of powers. Inasmuch as the Constitution sets up no such thing as an executive branch, we should acknowledge that in all major issues of management and policy the Congress and the President are jointly involved in the direction and control of the departments and agencies. There are frequent conflicts involved in the control of the departments between the Congress and the President or, more frequently, between some committee of the Congress and the President. But it is not a zero-sum game in which one side gains to the extent the other loses: the Congress as a whole may gain more effective control over the government, not by weakening the President, but only by delegating authority, with a proper measure of accountability, to him and his executive officers.

The proper extent of delegation from the Congress will determine the way in which the President, too, delegates to his department heads, and even to the staff in his Executive Office. The Congress may delegate either formally by statute or tacitly by refraining from interference. If it is to do so, it must develop a greater concentration of leadership and responsibility within each house, backed by more effective political discipline, so that it will have a stronger position in bargaining and negotiating with the President.

More coherent and effective leadership within each house of Congress, with stronger party discipline, would let the Congress as a whole (even if the two houses were not controlled by the President's party) bargain on equal or more than equal terms with the President on issues of sufficient importance to warrant the attention of the voters. Without it, as at present, the party rivalry turns on special issues generated by subcommittee oversight of particular bureaus or departments, and there is no way for the President to know on what policies the Congress as a whole will support him or for the public to be clear on what issues the next election should turn.

If such effective political leadership could be developed in the Congress as a whole, it might then be possible to focus responsibility on the executive side clearly on the department heads, to whom Congress by statute appropriates funds and grants the powers that operate directly on private citizens. That responsibility is now confused because of the growth in the size and glamor of the Executive Office. That growth has been far beyond the genuine interests of either the President or of the Congress as a whole; it has come about because special interests in both executive agencies and in congressional committees, many of them good in purpose, have sought to establish footholds at higher levels in the political hierarchy.[2]

There is no question that the President needs a strong Executive Office. His legal authority over the departments is guaranteed by his Constitutional power to dismiss their heads. But such authority is meaningless if it is not supported by staff resources and even more if it is not freed from undue statutory procedural constraints. The Executive Office was set up to provide the staff; if Congress is to be asked to leave it free from statutory constraints and at the President's discretion with respect to its organization and control, the President will need to live up to the tacit bargain on which the office was founded—that it not become a rival of the executive departments in the exercise of direct authority. For, unlike members of the Executive Office, the department head is not only directly responsible to the President, who may fire him, but he is also accountable to both the courts and the Congress, which may control the powers and the funds that are granted to him.

Various Presidents have come into office promising to make more effective use of their department heads—to strengthen "cabinet government" in the American sense of the term—and have drifted back to relying more on Executive Office staff, especially those in the White House. They have been tempted to do so because their department heads have been under congressional pressure less from the overall leadership, to which they could respond with some degree of unity as the principal members of the President's political team, than from the subcommittees and their staffs, which usually press them in the direction of their several special interests.

If there were some such effective congressional leadership it might be possible to raise the level of negotiation with the President from the details that have preoccupied committees and their staffs to more general questions of broad policy. Thomas Jefferson remarked that under the Articles of Confederation, "executive details" put us in the position "as if we had no federal head, by diverting the attention of that head from great to small subjects."[3] If there were more effective and disciplined leadership in the Congress, the bargaining between the leadership of the Congress and the President might be elevated to large subjects rather than the comparatively petty issues that dominate when the bargaining is between a congressional committee or its staff and a bureau chief.

There is no political force which can make such a change take place except a consensus based on the understanding and conviction of political leaders generally. The Congress, as noted in Chapter IV, amended the unwritten constitution during the mid-nineteenth century by taking away from the President the controls over the tools of administration—personnel, financial management, and organization—that had been conceded to him during the Federalist period. Then, with the Civil Service Act of 1883, the Budget and Accounting Act of 1921, and the Reorganization Act of 1939, it delegated these responsibilities back to the President—in limited ways and subject to careful checks. It can continue the process if it and the public understand the importance of doing so. It will not do to give up in impatience: it took nearly a half century to get a federal budget system after it was first discussed in congressional circles in the 1880s, and another half century for the Civil Service Reform Act of 1978 to be enacted after personnel reformers began to discuss the need for a higher civil service based on more general standards of competence and commitment.

THE LIMITS TO DELEGATION

When Congress delegated these responsibilities to the President, it had in mind that it was furthering efficiency in management rather than granting authority over the substance of policy. It is harder to delegate further to the President when the purpose is not efficiency in carrying out policies determined by legislation but the development of a more coherent policy.

Greater coherence is the ideal of those who would like to imitate the British parliamentary system and to move toward a single big check on the tenure of the executive. The parliamentary model, however, was never as persuasive with American public opinion as the model of the business corporation. If politics could be eliminated and government made to run like a business, with the President as general manager, the criterion of efficiency could guide public administration in the best utilitarian tradition. New intellectual support for the efficiency criterion has come from the applied social sciences: with cost-benefit analysis we should be able to calculate the choices involved in achieving the greatest good for the greatest number. But either the calculation of aggregate costs and benefits or the choice between the programs of two disciplined parties may ignore two crucial political values.

The first is the value of justice with respect both to fundamental rights and to the distribution of benefits and costs among the various regions and groups of the population. The Congress and the President will not want the secretary of defense, for example, to be able in his calculation of our military needs to ignore the civil rights of minority groups or even to allocate contracts without regard to the impact on various regions or segments of the economy. Nor will they want to let the administrator responsible for the protection of the environment ignore the special impact of particular regulations on particular industries or on employment opportunities.

The second is the value of freedom from arbitrary political power: a free people will prefer less bread and fewer circuses if the sacrifice will let them maintain more popular control over their own affairs.

Especially in a large federal system, with a diverse population, it is inevitable that the electorate will want to draw back from the idea of a tightly unified system in which the only check on the power that it delegates is by its choice between two political parties.[4] It is not only inevitable but desirable, in recognition of what history may teach us of the temptation of any political elite or any tightly organized bureaucracy to distort its perception of national policy in order to maintain its own profit and power. In a unitary state in an era of restricted governmental functions, a tightly unified and disciplined parliamentary system produced an admirably coherent policy. But it did so on a completely unscientific basis. In order to bring various groups together in teamwork, there is no way to calculate precisely, on a systematic utilitarian basis, just what choices will most fairly distribute benefits among them.[5] A somewhat looser system, in which parts of the majority may open issues up for public debate and independent voting in the legislature, may have its advantages.

Those advantages seem especially compelling since, in an era of government control over the economy and its technological development, it is hard for the political leader to be sure that his view of policy is based on a realistic comprehension of the scientific alternatives. He may be badly served if his own subordinates, either in political or career positions, do not fully comprehend what the technological options are or if they deliberately ignore some alternatives in order to push their own prejudiced views on policy. The possibility that better alternative choices may emerge from free-wheeling debate in an undisciplined legislature with free access to private scientific advice may be worth preserving even if it is less tidy than the classic parliamentary system of responsible government.

While it is important to have a government that can deal effectively with the great issues of the day, it is equally important to make sure that it does so in ways that take into account the essential moral and political values of justice and freedom. It is obviously essential to cope with the threat of war or of our loss of command of the sources of energy for our industrial system or of the deterioration of our environment. But these are special manifestations of a broader problem, namely, how can our political system insure that our ends are not corrupted by our means, that is to say, that our moral and political values control our technological and managerial skills and not vice versa. To this end, we must pay at least as much attention to insuring the accountability of our executive institutions as to improving their efficiency and economy. Indeed, we need to give prior attention to accountability, for it is the fear of irresponsible power that leads us to hobble our executives and destroy their effectiveness. Only by insuring their accountability will we be willing to grant them enough authority to act.

THE BASIS OF DELEGATION

In order to be held truly accountable, an executive—especially the President—needs to be given a greater degree of freedom in the formulation of policy. The major issues of the era cannot be defined and presented by the inspiration of a President alone: they require sustained staff study and careful consultation with responsible officials. The President, in dealing with the typical policy issue (as distinct from the conduct of diplomacy or military operations) should not be granted authority to make the final big decisions. But he does need to be given the opportunity to put before the Congress mature and careful proposals for Congress to reject, amend, or accept. This calls for giving the President more discretion in the procedures for the formulation and coordination of policy—for a greater measure of privacy and confidentiality in the preparation of staff papers and in the discussions in administrative committees than is permitted by statutes relating to the freedom of information or by the habits of the press and television. And it calls for greater freedom to be selective in the choice and timing of issues to be decided, which in turn would require more influence over the legislative agenda and more ability to withstand the pressures for action from publicity in the media.

The most cogent argument for the Congress to delegate in these ways a higher degree of discretion to the President is that it will enable both of them to give more weight to the ends of policy and the general values that determine them than to the technical means or to bureaucratic procedures. In ideal terms, this is the more democratic and responsible arrangement since it focuses the attention of the electorate and Congress as a whole on the main general issues, which they are interested in and competent to decide, rather than on technical or procedural details, which they are not.

If we are to manage to reconcile the utilitarian demand for efficiency with the protection of justice and freedom, it will not be easy to develop a system of accountability that permits so much political discretion on the part of either the President or congressional leaders. Our traditional political attitudes make it difficult. Americans distrust political authority and prefer to constrain power by scientific and legalistic standards. So we need to go back to the fourth basic question raised at the outset in the Introduction: on what type of knowledge may we base our approach to political responsibility, as well as to specific decisions of policy or administration? What, in short, is the basis of political authority and accountability?

The appeal to scientific or legal standards, as we have noted repeatedly, typically works in American politics in favor of the dispersion of authority and against the coordination of policy. It does so, however, in part—perhaps in major part—because the present procedures and institutions of the unwritten constitution encourage narrow special interests to appeal to science or the law. If those procedures and institutions, by general consent, came to emphasize a higher degree of delegation and a higher concentration of interest on the major issues of policy, both science and the law might well serve to support a more balanced type of accountability.

As for science, it is in its abstract basis a reductionist approach to knowledge, with no concern for values. As a result, it is true that a strictly scientific analysis of a current policy issue always leaves major questions to be answered by moral or political judgment. You can measure the contribution to the economy to be made by strip-mining new veins of coal more precisely than you can measure the damage to the environment, including its aesthetic costs. You can measure or estimate the lives that could be saved by requiring the use of seat belts in autos, but the costs in terms of personal freedom cannot be expressed statistically.

On the other hand, it is equally useless to try to decide any such issues solely on the basis of uninformed moral principles; the more difficult political problems are not those on which decisions can be made without regard for the costs or the physical difficulties involved. And when we move from current issues to the planning of future policies, the contribution of the sciences becomes even more essential. It is impossible to know what one should do without first finding out what one can do and what other goods must be sacrificed to do it. And it is often possible not only to calculate the trade-offs between competing goods but to discover ways to escape dilemmas and to integrate apparently conflicting purposes more intelligently so as to achieve them in harmony. If the United States is to develop a public service capable of transcending our policy dilemmas, scientists will have to play a major role in its composition and its procedures.[6]

As for the law, it is the necessary way to restrain the arbitrary and irresponsible use of power in the interest of political freedom for all. But it is also true that the control of government by highly detailed rules is the obvious line of defense by special interests against public authority. The special interests appeal to conceptions of justice that were founded on our public philosophy and, originally, on theological beliefs. That philosophy, however, may even more effectively support the general public interest as against special interests, but only if political institutions can raise the level of public attention to the major issues and if political leaders see their obligations to society in broader terms than the interests of local constituents or the enforcement of rigid specific rules.

The more important issues that arise at the higher levels of the governmental hierarchy are usually those involving conflicts among competing goods, on which decisions ought to be controlled in the end not by scientific data or predetermined rules but by moral and political judgment, guided in turn by a concern for the general welfare. The contrast between specific rules and general principles is an old and familiar one in theology and philosophy. From highly detailed codes of conduct to the obligation to love God and one's neighbor or from obedience to the commands of the sovereign to the philosopher's affirmation of the categorical imperative—this ascent from legalistic detail to a broader sense of ethical obligation rises to a higher standard of moral accountability. And it receives some concurrence, although perhaps not very broad popular support, from the belief that the advancement of science depends on the continuous discovery of broader and simpler principles of causal explanation.[7]

In legal theory a similar difference has existed between the legal positivists, who argue that law is a system of rules adopted by authority that are distinct from moral principles, and those who believe that the law is based also on fundamental rights, which are best expressed not in enforceable rules but in principles which may sometimes conflict with each other and have to be applied with political discretion. This latter emphasis on rights as having a basic validity apart from enacted law may well justify a system of accountability in which congressional leaders and the President leave many important decisions to be made by subordinates with a large measure of discretion, depending on the support of a political consensus not necessarily brought to formal votes.[8] A political decision can sometimes be made more responsibly without being expressed in a binding rule or a precise set of orders. An effective general policy cannot be outlined in detailed regulation without undesirable rigidities; a developing program needs to be based on cooperative consultation, guided by general political principles. The temptation to reduce such principles to binding rules—rules regarding either the substance of decisions or their procedures—is responsible for the excesses of bureaucratic red tape.

Moreover, accountability at high political levels cannot be assured by red tape. Politics is the art of agreeing on values and purposes in situations that are not covered by established law and that are too complex to be subject to measurement by recognized disciplines. Accountability must be a political matter to be worked out within the context of our unwritten constitution. It depends, not on precise Constitutional distinctions between the roles of the Congress and the President, but on political cooperation between them or on political controversy that illuminates broad issues and thus helps the voters make their fundamental decisions on election day as between competing candidates and parties.

To provide a proper measure of such accountability, the Congress would need to provide for a greater degree of party discipline. That would mean asking the electorate to delegate to the Congress a greater measure of responsibility, rather than following the reformist impulse that requires the instant reporting of every political negotiation and the independent voting of every member under the pressure of television commentators and special interest lobbies. With such political discipline, the Congress could delegate generally to the President the authority necessary for administrative coordination and management but still reserve to itself the right to intervene on some measures that it may consider important, especially if they involve questions of fundamental rights, distributive justice (such as the competing interests of the several regions), and political freedom. Such intervention, as a practical matter, requires the existence of congressional committees with the right to challenge the leadership of the parties or the President.

If one were to insist on achieving the full extent of party discipline and coherence of policy of the classic parliamentary system, it would be necessary to abolish such a role for committees, since their challenge to the cabinet in power would indicate a lack of the confidence on which the cabinet's tenure depends. But as long as the President and members of Congress have fixed and independent tenures, there is good reason to maintain the double channel of accountability, with the executive departments reporting primarily to the President but having to answer to congressional committees as well for their policies. This overlap can be a constructive and useful one, provided the committees themselves are made more accountable to the Congress as a whole, and their policies are effectively subject to review and reversal by congressional leadership in negotiation with the President.

For such a system to be tolerable, it is necessary to accept the idea that political authority, while it ought not to be absolute, need not be defined precisely in law. It needs, on the other hand, an understanding between the executive and the Congress with respect to ways in which accountability is to work in terms of organization and procedures. Like most important political issues, these arrangements are matters of balance and proportion. They can be worked out by political bargaining in the continuous process of revising the unwritten constitution, as the President and the Congress have been doing for many years.

This continuous revision, it must be admitted, has its costs. It makes it impossible for either the politician or the career officer to be certain at any point of crisis just where his responsibility lies. That is the difficulty of the American system by contrast with the British. On the other hand, as the British compared themselves a century or two ago with the more nearly absolute monarchies of Europe, their growing acceptance of the legitimacy of His Majesty's Loyal Opposition introduced uncertainties into the traditional ideas of obedience to royal authority. If, as a matter of degree, the Congress can move toward a somewhat more predictable and responsible system in its internal procedures and its relationship with the presidency, the United States might attain a tolerable balance, for a federal system in a technological era, in its system of accountability.

Most of the important issues on which the American system of accountability is constantly being revised are adjusted by informal consensus or procedural rules; few require statutory change, and none needs amendment of the written Constitution. A few examples may illustrate the point.

145

Number of Legislative Checks

For purposes of enforcing accountability, how many legislative check points are most effective? Under the classic parliamentary system the legislature has only one big check—to vote the government out of office. Under the congressional system, the legislature runs several simultaneous checks on each agency or program: legislative authorizations, appropriations, personnel ceilings, and a wide variety of oversight procedures—audits, reporting requirements, legislative vetoes, and scientific standards. How many different checks provide the optimum in accountability? The number of checks now provided is probably so great as to be counterproductive and serves no purpose except to enhance the influence of specific members or staff members of Congress. Indeed, the Congress—by having, for example, an authorizing committee seek to build up a program, an appropriations subcommittee cut it down, another committee control its organization or personnel, and a budget committee go over the whole sequence again—involves itself in levels of administrative detail that add nothing to its ability as a whole to control or to educate the public on major policy issues. But this issue is one of degree and proportion; just as Congress by creating the Congressional Budget Office not only put some restraint on the competing powers of various appropriations and budget and finance committees but also increased the effective accountability of the executive, so it might do more to cut down on the multiplicity and detail of its controls over the executive and consolidate its own effective power.

Legal or Political Checks

Are checks more effective when expressed in formal statutory terms or in less formal political understandings? Congressional committees, in their present relationship with executive bureaus, sometimes have enough confidence in the continuity of their relationships with career officers to be willing to define controlling decisions, not in rigid statutory terms, but in the legislative history as informal agreements. Presidents often object to this practice because it prevents them from coordinating policies. But if the less legalistic understandings were to be made between general congressional leadership, supported by political discipline, and the President, supported by a stronger career staff, the effect might be quite different. It would allow for greater executive discretion but subject it to more immediate political control.

Procedures for Initiative

Can procedures be devised to leave more flexible initiative in the hands of the President without weakening congressional control? The type of legislative veto that was originally devised to apply to reorganization plans seemed such a device. But there were Constitutional objections even to it, and they became stronger when the veto came to be exercised on detailed regulations and by a single house or committee of Congress. In the other direction, would something like an item veto for the President be desirable? Both approaches are worth exploring, provided that congressional action be taken by the political leadership of Congress as a whole.

Distinction Between Discussion and Determination of Policy

At what stage in the formulation and presentation of a new policy should accountability be exercised? If freedom of information is an absolute value or if it is often exercised by leaks to the press, it may be impossible for a policy to be developed into mature form for congressional consideration since special interests may more easily block its development by one political tactic or another.

This issue is especially significant if the President is to be encouraged to involve department heads more intimately in the formulation of policy through cabinet committees. Is accountability furthered by leaving the membership and agenda of such committees at the discretion of the President, as the first Hoover Commission recommended in 1949, or by subjecting them to public scrutiny and congressional control? Presidents are often reluctant to involve department heads in committee deliberation on major policy issues because it is difficult to keep such discussions confidential. They fear with some reason that Congress will undertake to decide what cabinet committees should exist, who should serve on them, and how they should operate. This fear may have justified the President

147

in relying more on Executive Office staff, and excluding department heads from the more important and confidential policy discussions.

It would make the entire process more responsible if Congress should act on what the President actually decides and recommends publicly, and leave to the discretionary management of the President the processes and procedures of preliminary thought within the Executive Office, the cabinet, and other interdepartmental committees.

Political and Career Staff

If accountability should be defined in terms, not of compliance with statutes or strict rules, but of conformity to general policy leadership and the broad intentions of the leadership, is such responsiveness more to be expected from political appointees or from career officers or from what kind of mix of both? The answer to this question will depend in part on the type of training and incentive system by which the higher civil service is developed. Will the new Senior Executive Service make a difference both by producing superior generalists and by making it easier for a President or a department head to bring to a particular position an officer responsive or congenial to his policies?

The rigidities of the old personnel system led political executives to want larger numbers of political appointees at the heads of their agencies. Yet, especially in the Executive Office, this approach had its limits. Political appointees (except for a few intimate friends) were usually less loyal to the President than to some special interest or faction that had promoted their appointment. As the Executive Office grew larger so that most of its staff had no personal contact with the President, the partisan loyalty of political appointments often proved less reliable than the professional loyalty of the career officer. As a matter of proportion, the Executive Office could well do with a much smaller number of political appointees as it did during its early years.

Size of the Executive Office

If the questions above can be answered, what do they imply for the size of the Executive Office? If the focus of accountability is to be on the executive departments, the Executive Office staff—even the institutional staffs—must be small enough so that its members can be close enough to the President so that they know his views intimately and can speak for him. On the other hand, that would call for a staff far too small to help the President respond to initiatives or questions from congressional staff now something like ten times as large as his own. A very large proportion—my guess is three-quarters to nine-tenths—of the time of the Executive Office staff and of congressional staff is spent in defensive maneuvers against each other, with no benefit either to the substance of policy or to accountability. If the original principles of the Executive Office are worth trying to reestablish, it might be necessary at the same time to reduce the size of the congressional as well as the Executive Office staffs so as to focus public and legislative attention on the major policy issues confronting the departments rather than on a mass of administrative details, especially those involved in services to constituents. We have learned that deregulation may improve the efficiency of private business; is it not possible that the executive departments could be made more efficient, with no loss of essential accountability in broad policy terms, if freed from some of the detailed regulation by the Executive Office and congressional staffs alike?

Adjustment Without Amendment

Those who drafted the Constitution of 1789 could not have foreseen some of these questions, but they would surely have been prudent enough not to try to answer them for all time in rigid legalistic terms. Their Constitution was more adaptable than the state constitutions of the preceding decade, when legislative supremacy was the ideal or than those adopted during the mid-nineteenth century, when the direct popular election of minor officers left both legislatures and governors incapable of dealing with the aggressive power of the great private corporations. The written Constitution of 1789 has been flexible enough to permit, within its formal framework, a higher degree of delegation by the electorate to the Congress and on in turn to the President. And such delegation has made possible the evolution of a richly varied unwritten constitution that can be adapted by political bargaining to new needs and circumstances.

Even though the United States abandoned the theory of sovereignty that Edmund Burke and other English traditionalists affirmed, in political practice Americans followed Burke in making their main adjustments in their unwritten constitution on the basis of Burke's "computing principle"—the unquantifiable process of working out "balances between differences of good; in compromises between good and evil, and sometimes between evil and evil. Political reason," he went on to say, "is a computing principle; adding, subtracting, multiplying, and dividing, morally, and not metaphysically or mathematically, true moral denominations."[9] Once we Americans lost our innocence about sovereignty—the kind of innocence that, as Walter Bagehot argued, made the parliamentary system possible by letting most people know only the "dignified" parts of the constitution while practical politicians in the Cabinet controlled its "efficient" parts[10]—the only way to reestablish a workable authority was by delegation on the computing principle.

In this approach, the Americans and the British were closer to each other than to continental Europe. Both came to believe in the most fundamental kind of separation of powers in their political systems, namely, the separation of the institutions that wielded political power from those concerned with the search for truth, whether on a religious or a scientific basis.

This separation originated in fundamental beliefs but effectively depended on institutional habits. The fundamental belief of the Puritan dissenters in the depravity of mankind made it hard to maintain an institutional structure with absolute political authority. This was not because they were consistent in applying their beliefs; in the seventeenth century John Milton was already attacking the Puritans for trying to be as authoritarian as the papists: in his words, "New *Presbyter* is but old *Priest* writ large."[11] But without either a traditional establishment or a theology that justified hierarchical authority, the Puritan commonwealths collapsed—rejected in England by the Stuart restoration and in New England by the competition of other dissenting denominations. From that time on, the English-speaking world—having been, so to speak, politically inoculated—was comparatively immune to the virus of a tyranny based on confidence either in the old priesthood or in the new kind based on faith in science. Comte and Marx and their followers were never able to exercise the influence on the evolution of political ideas that they had on the Continent, especially in Eastern Europe. But in Britain the persistence of an establishment—not only the established churches of England and Scotland but the civil service establishment and the tight unity of policy that it maintained in support of a conservative class structure—gave the doctrines of Marx a chance to gain a modest foothold in the Labour party, although never to the extent of making a proletarian dictatorship in the slightest degree plausible.

Britain and America were rather more vulnerable to the rival doctrine of perfectibility—the belief of Herbert Spencer and William Graham Sumner that the advancement of science would lead to general happiness and prosperity if only government would avoid interfering with the economy. This belief may have been useful as an insurance against undue concentration of power: if the sciences had not been established and supported on the institutional patterns set by the religious dissenters, there might have been some danger of the development of the new scientific priesthood that Comte hoped for and Spencer and Huxley feared.

The Spencer-Sumner doctrine, however, had its costs, especially in the United States where it was taken more seriously than in Britain. It was a belief that ignored the need of modern technological society for some authority to reconcile conflicting class interests and assure justice to the poor. This belief was taken as an excuse for the lack of a tradition of public service in the wealthier class of American citizens. And it made very difficult the development of an administrative service that could maintain the supremacy of general political values over the competing scientific specialties and thus provide the basis for a more effective system of political accountability.

To establish the kind of accountability that is necessary in the constitutional system of the United States today, it is essential to avoid a legalistic worship of the ancient text and to look at the more important political issues of the unwritten constitution. If we fix our attention on that aspect of our problem, we may still learn useful lessons from those who drafted the Constitution of 1789. For the general attitude they brought to the Constitutional Convention was one that is still appropriate: political responsibility depends on the recognition that the duties of political leadership and public administration are the most important obligations of the citizen, and call for the dedication of the highest talents in society. And the specific insight that they had learned from painful experience with the Articles of Confederation may still be useful: a republican policy without a monarchical or bureaucratic establishment to give it stability will do well to have a chief executive and a legislative body with fixed and independent tenures.

The relationship that such an arrangement encourages is a partial protection not only against the disintegration of the executive by the distracting loyalties of legislators to their local constituents, but also against the corruption of Congress by presidential pressure or patronage. Even more important, it serves a purpose that the United Kingdom may need less than the United States, where we maintain a more naïve and literal faith in the direct application of religion or science to public policy: it helps to define the boundary between government and the established institutions of education and research, as well as those of religion. And along this line of mutual defense, it is sometimes the politicians who are more in need of protection from aggression.

References and Reminiscences

As noted at the end of the Preface, the remaining pages, which indicate the sources from which the text of the book was drawn, include not only the conventional references to documents and other publications but also reminiscences of the personal experiences which were responsible, to an even greater degree, for the opinions and prejudices that show through any scholarly work. They are arranged in the order of the chapters to which they refer.

Introduction. The Confused Sources of Authority

My interest in comparing English and American politics began at the age of eight. My home was in a mountain town in southeastern Kentucky, just north of Cumberland Gap, which had been developed in the 1880s by Baring Brothers and other English capitalists as a center for new coal and iron mining development. The area was, in economic terms, an English colony; most of the land in several counties around was owned (and still is) by a London corporation, and while the labor for the coal mines had been recruited from the surrounding hills, the managers and lawyers had been imported not only from other parts of the United States but also from Great Britain and Canada.

While most (though not all) of the foreigners had given up and gone home after the depression of 1893, the cultural influence of the English remained. In my grandfather's home there was a great collection of books that, a generation earlier, he had bought or borrowed from his English colleagues for my uncles to read. These were stories about public school life in England, which I read with avid interest as soon as I learned to read at all. There were many things about them I found incomprehensible, aside from the fact that by "public school" they meant private school. The most memorable general point was that invariably, when a young gentleman student at the "public" school had a fight with a lower-class bully, the young gentleman won.

This was not my experience in the public school of Middlesboro, Kentucky. The coal miners' sons were as big and strong as the sons of lawyers and managers and very much rougher and tougher. My grandfather was a lawyer, state legislator, and judge, and deeply interested in politics. We spent every Sunday afternoon at his home, where the family conversation was always about politics. The side he took in local politics was invariably beaten by the majority that was dominated by the local mountaineers. So I grew up wondering wistfully how in England the educated elite managed to control the government, as well as to dominate games on the school playground.

My family, immigrants to the mountains from central Kentucky and the North, were Democrats. The county had voted Federalist, Whig, and Republican since 1796 with never a break, usually by a majority of ten to one or better. During the 1920s, we were in a political minority locally, and the local Republicans were in a minority in Democratic Kentucky, which was in a minority nationally during the Republican years of Harding to Hoover. My political attitudes were consequently shaped by the habit of disagreeing with authority, but in an attitude of weary and cynical resignation rather than useless rebellion—the ideal emotional preparation for the civil service.

In more liberal times and places, my contemporaries were taught that religion and politics ought to be kept separate and often assumed that they actually were. On the factual (as against the ideal) issue I was never misled. My Presbyterian family knew that the county was controlled politically by the Baptists, with a small leavening of Holy Rollers. A few miles to the east, in the southwestern tip of Virginia, the Methodists had a foothold. While working in that area one summer in a limestone quarry, trying to earn college tuition, I found that in a town of some two hundred population there were two Methodist churches, the Methodist Episcopal Church, North, and the M.E. Church, South. I asked why. With pity for my naïve ignorance, my local co-worker said, "Why, of course, we have to have one church for the Republican Methodists and one for the Democrat Methodists."

My early upbringing gave me a lively interest in both the contrasts between English and American political habits, and the ways in which they were influenced by the role of religious institutions.

1. For example, see "Report of the Special Committee [headed by B. Carroll Reece] to Investigate Tax-Exempt Foundations and Comparable Organizations," *House Reports*, 83rd Cong., 2nd Sess., No. 2681 (1954), esp. 17–19, 422–25.
2. Yaron Ezrahi, "Einstein and the Light of Reason," in Gerald Holton and Yehuda Elkana (eds.), *Albert Einstein: Historical and Cultural Perspectives* (Princeton, 1982).
3. Some of the various approaches of this type are summarized in Thomas K. Finletter, *Can Representative Government Do the Job?* (New York, 1945), Chap. 13, and Edward S. Corwin, *The President: Office and Powers* (New York, 1957), esp. 296–99, 487–91.
4. For an analysis of the decay in Great Britain of the old unity and discipline of the political parties, see Samuel H. Beer, *Britain Against Itself: The Political Contradictions of Collectivism* (New York, 1982).

Chapter I. Saints and Scientists

My approach to this subject was influenced, some years before any practical experience in government, by an education that was quite different from that of the typical social scientist of today: in literature and history. At Vanderbilt University, where I took the first of my three academic degrees (all of them bachelor's degrees), my main interests were in English literature. The leading professors there were the southern agrarian poets led by John Crowe Ransom and Donald Davidson. They left me with a sentimental interest in the traditional and religious roots of politics and some skepticism about the inevitability of progress based on technological and industrial development. My interest in literature was strong enough to deflect me from following the family tradition and becoming a lawyer, but not enough to make me want an academic career: I settled for journalism.

The result was a couple of newspaper jobs, one in the summer on the daily newspaper in my small home town, one in Nashville. The purpose of both was to earn enough money to get through college in ways rather more pleasant than my earlier manual labor in the coal mines and the rock quarries; their effect was to temper my sentimental confidence in the neo-Confederate tradition and give me some hints about the influence of science in the modern world. The Nashville newspaper on which I worked was in bankruptcy and its publisher in the North Carolina penitentiary for financial manipulation of local government budgets. My coverage of state politics, in which Boss Crump of Memphis maintained power by tactics that had little to do with the idealism of my poetic mentors, persuaded me that there were some new aspects of southern society that an idealistic education had not covered.

Vanderbilt as a university illustrated some of those aspects. Its most influential segments were not those derived from the Methodist background or its literary fame. Its chancellor had indeed broken its ties with the Methodist church in order to develop it as an independent secular university. Later, with the help of the foundations supporting medical education along the lines proposed by the famous Flexner Report, he had built up its medical school into its most prosperous faculty and had supported the scientific departments in fighting the segments of opinion in Tennessee that had backed William Jennings Bryan and the prosecution of Scopes for the teaching of evolution in the public schools of Dayton, Tennessee. More than a half century before the debates about "creationism," Vanderbilt as a southern university was strongly committed on the side of the scientists.

My newspaper jobs continued during my senior year in college and for a full year thereafter, but during that period I was lucky enough to be awarded a Rhodes Scholarship. The chairman of the regional selection committee in Atlanta was a newspaper publisher who was a bitter enemy of my Nashville employer; I have always suspected that he decided to rescue a nice young man from evil connections, without too much regard for scholarly merit.

At Oxford, still having a newspaper career in mind, I intended to study in the most modern of the Honours Schools (philosophy, politics, and economics), but Merton College was too small to have a tutor in such a new approach to education. The senior tutor, Idris Deane Jones, was a historian, who persuaded me to take the Modern History Honours School instead. Even though "modern" history then ended in 1870, I have never regretted the decision; it gave me a perspective on the United Kingdom that I would never have acquired by a branch of study more social-scientific in nature.

Deane Jones was a specialist in Byzantine history, and interested in the ways in which the Eastern Orthodox and the Roman Catholic churches by their conflict had influenced the political history of Western Europe. He made it easy to translate this interest into a concern for more recent religious dissent and its political consequences. When I was required to choose a special subject to prepare for the final examinations, I chose the seventeenth-century Puritan revolution and became intrigued by the way in which it had developed a line of constitutional thinking that the restoration of the monarchy and the established Anglican church had foreclosed for the British forever.

I retained an interest in the contrast between the United Kingdom's unwritten parliamentary constitution and a federal system with a formal constitution, but I got little sympathy on this subject from my tutor, even though he was a Welshman and in a sentimental way an Anglophobe. I recall one session under his tutelage with a fellow student—years later a Tory whip in the House of Commons—who had read his John Richard Green and alluded to the "Anglo-Saxon genius for self-government." Our tutor asked bitterly whether he, as a Celt, and I, as an American of uncertain and obviously mongrel ancestry, had to look to an Englishman as the only one capable of self-government.

But he never showed any interest in the possibilities of regional devolution; I wonder whether he would not have been pleased by the popular discussion of that possibility a half century later. And the world of science and technology was quite outside his range. I would not have known that they existed at Oxford but for my occasional work "on the string" as a reporter for the Associated Press. I can recall being mystified by my interview of Frederick Soddy, the great physicist, who tried to give me some hint of the future exploration of the atomic nucleus, but found it all beyond my comprehension.

1. Michael Walzer, *The Revolution of the Saints* (Cambridge, Mass., 1975), tells the story of the Puritan rebellion and interprets its consequences.
2. Charles Francis Adams (ed.), *The Works of John Adams* (Boston, 1850–56), III, 453–54.
3. John Calvin, *Institutes of the Christian Religion* (Philadelphia, n.d.), I, 90.
4. Sydney E. Ahlstrom, *A Religious History of the American People* (New Haven, 1972), 305.
5. A. D. Lindsay, *The Modern Democratic State* (Oxford, 1943), I, 118. The debates are recounted from the Clarke Papers in A. S. P. Woodhouse, *Puritanism and Liberty* (London, 1938).

6. Thomas Carlyle (ed.), *Oliver Cromwell's Letters and Speeches* (New York, 1856), II, 120–21.

7. The story from a resentful Scottish point of view is told by Bruce Lenman, *The Jacobite Risings in Britain, 1689–1746* (London, 1980), esp. 34, 73, 105.

8. Caroline Robbins, *The Eighteenth-Century Commonwealthman* (Cambridge, Mass., 1961).

9. *Ibid.*, 266.

10. Ernest Barker, "A Huguenot Theory of Politics," in Barker, *Church, State, and Education* (Ann Arbor, 1957), 81–101.

11. The Hollis story is told not only by Robbins, *The Eighteenth-Century Commonwealthman*, but also by Barker, *Church, State, and Education*, 101, and by Perry Miller, *The New England Mind: From Colony to Province* (Cambridge, Mass., 1953), 444, 456. Miller also tells how Cotton Mather, disgruntled by the theological and political developments at Harvard, tried unsuccessfully to persuade Hollis to give the divinity chair to Yale after successfully persuading Elihu Yale to turn his benefactions there.

12. Charles Webster, *The Great Instauration* (London, 1975), 27, and generally in Chaps. I, V, and VI; Robert K. Merton, *Science, Technology, and Society in Seventeenth-Century England* (New York, 1970).

13. Eric Ashby, *Technology and the Academics* (London, 1959), Chap. 1.

14. Robbins, *The Eighteenth-Century Commonwealthman*, 336.

15. Henry F. May, *The Enlightenment in America* (New York, 1976), 219–22.

16. Henri Laboucheix, *Richard Price* (Montreal [1970?]), 29–44. Price, as an early social scientist, was an early victim of the temptations of his successors. His statistics were sometimes biased by his political prejudices, and by emphasizing scientific method, he sometimes ignored the essential policy problem. Turgot, who had lost his position as controller of finance for the King of France, wrote to Price that his calculations failed to take into account the complexity of the real world, and that "cette science approfondie serait plus intéressante pour les philosophes qu'importante pour les politiques" (33 n).

17. Richard Price, *Observations on the Nature of Civil Liberty, the Principles of Government, and the Justice and Policy of the War with America* (1776; rpr., Dunderave Ltd., 1976), esp. 8–9, 12–13, 15, 99–100.

18. Edmund Burke, "Reflections on the Revolution in France, and on the Proceedings of Certain Societies in London Relative to That Event," in *The Works of the Right Honourable Edmund Burke* (London, 1934), IV, 83. Price responded to this attack in 1790 in the preface to the fourth edition of *A Discourse on the Love of our Country*.

19. Bernard Bailyn, *Pamphlets of the American Revolution, 1750–1776* (Cambridge, Mass., 1965), I, 93, and Samuel H. Beer, "Federalism, Nationalism, and Democracy in America," *American Political Science Review*, LXXII, No. 1. Samuel P. Huntington, *Political Order in Changing Societies* (New Haven, 1968), Chap. 2, discusses this split in political tradition. Propagandists of the American Revolution, such as Joseph Hawley, argued strongly that Americans should "never more be puzzled and plagued with the jargon of virtual representation." Alan Heimert, *Religion and the American Mind* (Cambridge, Mass., 1966), 523.

20. It will be clear that I am more inclined to accept the constitutional theory of L. S. Amery's *Thoughts on the Constitution* (London, 1947) than the tradition from Bagehot to Harold Laski.

21. May, *The Enlightenment in America*, 278–302; *Adams Family Correspondence* (Cambridge, Mass., 1963), II, 45.

22. Jefferson's compilation from the New Testament, which he entitled *The Life and Morals of Jesus of Nazareth*, was in parallel columns in four languages,

Greek, Latin, French, and English. It was published in 1904 by the U. S. Government Printing Office.

23. May, *The Enlightenment in America*, Chap. 6.

24. A general comparison of the status of science in America in the eighteenth and nineteenth centuries is given by I. Bernard Cohen in "Science and American Society in the First Century of the Republic" (Alpheus W. Smith Lecture at the Graduate School, Ohio State University, Columbus, 1961).

25. Perry Miller, *The New England Mind: The Seventeenth Century* (Cambridge, Mass., 1954), 216–17.

26. Ahlstrom, *Religious History of the American People*, 306; Heimert, *Religion and the American Mind*, 59–61, 74–75. Passage quoted is from Edwards' private notebooks, quoted in C. C. Goen, "Jonathan Edwards: A New Departure in Eschatology," *Church History*, XXVIII (March, 1959), 29.

27. Ahlstrom, *Religious History of the American People*, 306, 351; Miller, *The New England Mind: From Colony to Province*, 442.

28. Heimert, *Religion and the American Mind*, 74–75.

29. This general point is made by Heimert, *Religion and the American Mind*, 304, 512–20. In general agreement are May, *The Enlightenment in America*, and Ahlstrom, *Religious History of the American People*, 363–64.

30. J. R. Pole, *The Pursuit of Equality in American Society* (Berkeley, 1978), 79–83.

31. William Ellery Channing, *Religion a Social Principle, a Sermon Delivered in the Church in Federal Street, Boston, Dec. 10, 1820* (Boston, 1820), 16–19. I am indebted to James Luther Adams for calling this sermon to my attention.

32. Ann Douglas, *The Feminization of American Culture* (New York, 1977), 26.

33. These points were elaborated by James Freeman Clarke in a sermon, *The Five Points of Calvinism and the Five Points of the New Theology* (Boston, 1885).

34. May, *The Enlightenment in America*, 332, 351, 406 n, 407 n. The story of Transylvania is also told in Niels Henry Sonne, *Liberal Kentucky* (New York, 1959).

35. Nathan O. Hatch, "The Christian Movement and the Demand for a Theology of the People," *Journal of American History*, LXVII (December, 1980).

36. Some family records allege that an ancestor of mine, a Moravian preacher, left Somerset County in western Pennsylvania with many relatives and friends after taking part in the Whiskey Rebellion of 1794, in which one of them "became a martyr to the cause of democracy," and settled in Kentucky. Such a normally unreliable piece of family tradition is given some plausibility by Alan Heimert's account of the Whiskey Rebellion (*Religion and the American Mind*, 547), and by the contemporary memoir of the region regarding the connection between evangelical theology and anti-Federalist politics: Daniel Drake, M.D., *Pioneer Life in Kentucky, 1785–1800* (New York, 1948).

37. Whitney R. Cross, *The Burned-Over District* (New York, 1965).

38. Perry Miller, *The Life of the Mind in America* (New York, 1965), 59.

39. Alexis de Tocqueville, *Democracy in America* (New York, 1900), Chap. XVII, pp. 304–306.

40. George Armstrong Kelly, "Faith, Freedom, and Disenchantment: Politics and the American Religious Consciousness," *Daedalus* (Winter, 1982), 127–48. For comments on America's "civil religion," see in the same *Daedalus* Dick Anthony and Thomas Robbins, "Spiritual Innovation and the Crisis of American Civil Religion," 215–34.

41. George Bancroft, *History of the United States of America from the Discovery of the Continent* (New York, 1888); Ernst Troeltsch, *Protestantism and Progress* (Boston, 1958; first English translation, 1912); H. Richard Niebuhr, *The Social Sources of Denominationalism* (New York, 1929).

42. R. H. Knapp and H. B. Goodrich, *Origins of American Scientists* (Chicago, 1952). The tendency of those with rigorous systematic minds to desert the clergy as a profession and the alliance of the remainder with mild and uncritical reform causes are described in Douglas, *Feminization of American Culture*.

43. Max Weber, *The Protestant Ethic and the Spirit of Capitalism*, trans. Talcott Parsons (London, 1930), and R. H. Tawney, *Religion and the Rise of Capitalism* (New York, 1926), are among the most influential. Weber's heavy emphasis on the economic aspects of behavior led him to say less about the effect of religious ideas on political behavior, as noted by James Luther Adams, "Mediating Structures and the Separation of Powers," in Michael Novak (ed.), *Democracy and Mediating Structures* (Washington, D.C., 1979).

44. Walzer, *The Revolution of the Saints*. Troeltsch, a contemporary of Weber, seems to me to take Walzer's side of the argument by giving priority in his *Protestantism and Progress*, 113–15, to the political over the economic influence of Calvinism. "Calvinism gave a much more radical development to its Law of Nature . . . established the principle of the right of resistance . . . tendency toward progress . . . specifically Reformed idea of the State . . . the idea of the State-contract." James Luther Adams suggests in "Mediating Structures and the Separation of Powers" that Weber may have intended in a later work to correct the balance by writing another study of the effect of religious ideas, this time on political behavior.

45. Gerald Holton, *The Scientific Imagination* (Cambridge, 1978), Chap. 7.

Chapter II. The Dissenting Establishment

Oxford influenced my later political thinking less by the teaching in its formal Honours School than by its general environment, and by the opportunity I found in my third year to get in touch with the way career civil servants saw their roles in politics.

The university and its colleges still showed traces of the old ecclesiastical establishment which had governed them for centuries. Merton College still maintained the formality of compulsory chapel at eight each morning, but in order to tolerate the consciences of dissenters without giving them an easier life, it permitted each undergraduate to get up at the same hour and, in academic gown, sign a book in the college offices. The old rules of the monastic establishment were still honored in form, but without undue conscientious rigor. The college gates were locked each evening at nine, but the more acrobatic undergraduates were well acquainted with the parts of the college wall that could be climbed by those of moderate sobriety. My tutor tried to make clear to me the main theoretical difference between the British respect for authority, or at least formal deference to authority, and the American legalistic and moralistic ways of thought. "You American students never seem to understand," he told me in our first interview. "Merton College has no rule against climbing into the college after midnight. It has a very strict rule against getting caught climbing into the college after midnight."

Then, for one later concerned with the subordination of the civil service to cabinet ministers, it was instructive to observe the deference of the college servants to the undergraduates, the young gentlemen whom the servants always addressed as "sir" but then undertook to instruct on points of conduct and etiquette. To me this deference seemed distasteful as a perpetuation of an obsolete class system. It took me some time to realize that a substantial proportion of the "young gentlemen" undergraduates, much larger than at any American university, were supported by governmental scholarships and, in terms of economic class, were from the same levels as the college servants.

The remnants of Victorian or even of medieval flavor were the main subject matter of the stories I filed as a "stringer" correspondent for the Associated Press—a half century later, American newspapers still carry articles by Rhodes scholars at Oxford on some of the same quaint customs. But once or twice a more significant story broke. I went to the Oxford Union—the debating society that has been training ground for generations of future members of the House of Commons—to cover the debate in 1933 on the subject "Resolved that this House will in no circumstances fight for its King and Country." The debate brought into focus the passionate pacifism of a whole generation who had heard or read of the misery of the deadlock in the trenches of Flanders, and the favorable vote on the resolution led many—some suggested, even Adolf Hitler—to believe that the Nazis need not fear military resistance from the United Kingdom.

There were various lessons to be learned later from that episode on the British and European side of the story, including the way in which one of the most passionate pacifists among the undergraduate speakers later joined the Royal Air Force and won a Victoria Cross as a bomber pilot. My own narrower lesson had to do with the way in which the habits of the American press affected political thinking. I telephoned the story that evening to the London AP office, and after giving the conclusion of the debate said to the desk man, "Hold on, this doesn't tell you much about the attitudes to King and Country of English youth. I could count among the majority far more than enough Americans, Indians, and Irishmen to determine the outcome." The desk man was unimpressed; that point, he thought, would ruin the story, and so it was never reported to an American public already inclined to believe in the decadence of English youth. If that Oxford Union vote did influence Hitler's thinking, the habits of journalists must bear some responsibility.

In my third year at Oxford, having finished the B.A. in modern history, I wanted to do some work that would let me learn more about contemporary government. Felix Frankfurter, on leave from Harvard Law School, had been on a one-year guest professorship at Oxford, and I had been intrigued by his lectures and discussions on the peculiarities (from the American point of view) of administrative and constitutional law in the United Kingdom, and especially on the authority and status of the higher civil service. I proposed accordingly to do a one-year research degree on that subject (the B.Litt., equivalent to something between an American M.A. thesis and a lesser Ph.D. thesis without the related disciplinary training).

I had the good luck to be put under the supervision of Sir Arthur (later Lord) Salter, who had just come to All Souls College from a distinguished career in the civil service. He exemplified the intellectual approach of the generalist in government—a contempt for highly specialized requirements, and an emphasis on personal independence and responsibility. At my first discussion with him, I tried to show that I had heard in America of the requirements for graduate research, and so I asked questions about methodology and especially about bibliographical and footnote requirements. He was uninterested: he pulled several books at random off the shelves and said, "All of these have footnotes; follow the style of any of them you like." And when, in order to narrow my subject to manageable scope, I suggested that I write a thesis on the Establishments Division of the Treasury—a unit that covered a range of issues controlled in the United States by the Budget Bureau and the Civil Service Commission put together—he was incredulous: "That," he remarked, "is a subject about which you could learn all you want to know in a couple of weeks. Why not take on something to stretch your powers? Write a comparative study of British and American government as a whole." I gulped and negotiated something halfway between: a study of the higher civil service in the two countries, with respect to their constitutional status, their relation to political authority, and their educational preparation and internal administration.

At the end of that discussion I asked when I should see him again, expecting him to say next week. "Well," he said, "this is late September; why don't you come back the end of November?" In the meantime I was on my own, working in government offices and libraries in London as well as at Oxford in ways that my journalistic experience, more than my academic education, encouraged me to do.

Aside from these general attitudes, his specialized interests and background made his counsel peculiarly useful to me. He had been the top career officer in the British-American joint administration of shipping control during the First World War, and his book *Allied Shipping Control* was a classic. It made clear the difference between the processes of legislation and of administrative coordination, with administrative committees having to work within the limits of existing authority but legislative committees having to make new law. I began dimly to perceive some ideas unfamiliar to those whose assumptions about committees are shaped by U.S. congressional procedures—how it is that the British Cabinet can make decisions without voting, and committees of British civil servants can be expected, more than occasionally, to seek to make effective policy compromises rather than (as in the U.S.) to stall on every issue and leak their conflicts to the press or legislators.

I was happy some years later to work for Sir Arthur Salter when he was deputy director general of the United Nations Relief and Rehabilitation Administration. I was on loan to it ("seconded," as the British say), in uniform, from the U.S. coast guard, the first such officer detailed by a military service to any United Nations agency, to help set up its international personnel system. It soon became apparent, as I dealt with the Russian high officials in UNRRA, that differences in political theory and in constitutional systems made it difficult to carry on the congenial type of committee coordination that Salter exemplified and that I had come to believe in. But more on that point may come in the notes to the next chapter.

1. Max Weber, *The Protestnt Ethic and the Spirit of Capitalism*, trans. Talcott Parsons (London, 1930).
2. Cotton Mather, *Magnalia Christi Americana*, ed. Kenneth B. Murdock (Cambridge, Mass., 1977), 143.
3. Alan Heimert, *Religion and the American Mind* (Cambridge, Mass., 1966), 458–59, discusses the way in which Jonathan Edwards' doctrine of liberty (as the "demanding, but not externally coercive, law of love") became identified with the law of nature and with rebellion against English law.
4. The Confession of Faith and the two Catechisms adopted by the Westminster Assembly during the Puritan Commonwealth of the 1640s and later approved by the Scottish General Assembly said that the "only two sacraments ordained by Christ our Lord in the gospel" were baptism and the Lord's supper. These documents, with only slight revisions to remove any trace of Erastian doctrine (*i.e.*, the doctrine of the subordination of the church to government) were adopted by the first Presbyterian synod in North America at Philadelphia in 1729; with a few slight revisions they may be found in most Presbyterian churches today.
5. Daniel J. Boorstin, *The Lost World of Thomas Jefferson* (New York, 1948), 225.
6. Perry Miller, *The New England Mind: From Colony to Province* (Cambridge, Mass., 1953), 365, 381, 441, 462.
7. Alexis de Tocqueville, *Democracy in America* (New York, 1900), Chap. XVII.
8. Raymond B. Fosdick, *The Story of the Rockefeller Foundation* (New York, 1952), Chaps. 1 and 2; Burton J. Hendrick, *The Life of Andrew Carnegie* (London, 1933). Both books discuss the key essay by Andrew Carnegie, "The Gospel of Wealth," *North American Review*, 1899. The story of the decision to support a program of university fellowships rather than to build up separate research institutions is told in Nathan Reingold, "The Case of the Disappearing Laboratory," *American Quarterly*, XXIX (Spring, 1977), 79–101.
9. Robert E. Kohler, "The Management of Science: The Experience of Warren Weaver and the Rockefeller Foundation Programme in Molecular Biology," *Minerva*, XIV (Autumn, 1976).
10. For an account of his wavering on the key issue of degree of accountability of science to politics—*i.e.*, whether the head of the proposed national foundation for the support of science should be appointed by the President—see J. Merton England, "Dr. Bush Writes a Report: Science the Endless Frontier," *Science*, January 9, 1976, pp. 45–46.
11. H. Richard Niebuhr, *The Social Sources of Denominationalism* (New York, 1929), Chap. IV.
12. E. O. Wilson, *On Human Nature* (Cambridge, Mass., 1978).
13. Alexandra Oleson and John Voss (eds.), *The Organization of Knowledge in Modern America, 1860–1920* (Baltimore, 1979), 107–58.
14. Edmund Burke, "Speech on Conciliation with the Colonies," in *Burke's Speeches and Letters on American Affairs* (London, 1931), 95.

15. Puritan theologians were painfully aware of the dangers of antinomian theology, which seemed to them to deny all moral laws by excessive emphasis on salvation by grace; they knew the story of the Anabaptists of Munster, who in the sixteenth century brought about anarchy and then tyranny in pursuit of an impossible ideal. That story is told in Norman Cohn, *The Pursuit of the Millennium* (New York, 1957).

16. The major exceptions are Cambridge, Mass., with its heavy academic influence, and the state of Maine, which was settled too late to be dominated by the Congregational establishment. In Cambridge, reform groups insisted on defining the conditions of tenure of the manager by detailed laws, thus violating the general principles of the plan that emphasized the full political responsibility of the council.

17. Walter Bagehot, *The English Constitution* (1867; rpr. Oxford, 1933), 232–33.

18. Virginia, where the Anglican tradition retained its influence on the institutional habits of community leaders until well along in the twentieth century, provided some conspicuous exceptions. Almost all of the towns where the system was adopted accorded the managers a quite un-American degree of respect and stability of tenure. See the studies of Fredericksburg and Lynchburg in Harold A. Stone, Don K. Price, and Kathryn H. Stone, *City Manager Government in Nine Cities* (Chicago, 1940).

19. L. Pearce Williams, *Michael Faraday* (New York, 1964).

20. Anson Phelps Stokes, *Church and State in the United States* (New York, 1950), III, 169.

21. Out of this movement, which its detractors called "Campbellite," grew a wide variety of independent churches, called variously the Disciples of Christ, the Christian Church, and the Churches of Christ. The most comprehensive and sympathetic account is in Winfred Ernest Garrison, *An American Religious Movement* (St. Louis, 1945). See pp. 88–89 for an account of Virginia Constitutional Convention, and pp. 106, 114, for Bacon College. For an account of the political conflicts between Campbell and the Presbyterians and Baptists, see Walter Brownlow Posey, *Religious Strife on the Southern Frontier* (Baton Rouge, 1965).

22. Stuart S. Blume, *Toward a Political Sociology of Science* (New York, 1974). A more recent list of societies of scientists especially concerned about nuclear disarmament is in *Science, Technology, and Human Values* (Fall, 1981), 26.

23. Howard Phillips, "Let's De-Fund the Left," *Conservative Digest* (April, 1982), 50.

24. Sidney H. Aronson, *Status and Kinship in the Higher Civil Service* (Cambridge, Mass., 1964), esp. 126–27, 129–34.

25. E. R. Norman, *Church and Society in England, 1770–1970* (Oxford, 1976), esp. 8–12, discusses the extent to which the Church of England clergy owed their social ideas to an ordinary university education rather than any specialized theological study.

26. Institute of Medicine, National Academy of Sciences, *Food Safety Policy: Scientific and Societal Considerations* (March 1, 1979). A more fundamental exploration of the general problem was undertaken by a study in 1981 by the Committee on Risk and Decision-Making of the National Research Council. That committee undertook to categorize and explain the difficulties involved in applying scientific methods to social problems.

Chapter III. Social Perfectibility and Human Engineering

Some of us very young liberals in the early 1930s assumed that, if selfish economic interests could be overridden and rational scientific ideas could prevail, the world would make progress perpetually. Even for one who was mainly interested in American domestic politics, it was hard to avoid being shaken during those years by the upheavals in Europe. For a backwoods boy like me it was an unusual education to see in the flesh all three of the great twentieth-century dictators—to hear Hitler harangue his followers in a Munich beer hall and Mussolini address the Fascist faithful from the portico of the Palazzo Venezia and then to see the embalmed Lenin on display in Red Square before endless files of Marxist worshippers. The Oxford vacations totaled twenty-eight weeks each year, and travel on the Continent was cheap; so even one living exclusively on a scholarship could wander about Europe carrying a bag full of books to be studied in preparation for the next examinations.

I was not alone among American Rhodes scholars whose future ideas and careers may have been influenced by the shock of observing the competing theories of tyranny. I spent some days in Berlin the summer after Hitler's takeover with Dean Rusk, who was specializing in German studies and looking forward to an academic career, and James McCormack, a West Point graduate who later became an Air Force Major General and headed the weapons development program of the Atomic Energy Commission a few years before Rusk was secretary of state. Then I shared a trip through Russia in the summer of 1934 with, among others, Charles J. Hitch, later the assistant secretary of defense who developed McNamara's program planning and budgeting system on the basis of his earlier work in the Rand Corporation, and Howland H. Sargeant, later assistant secretary of state and the head of Radio Liberty, the private corporation broadcasting (with government support) to the Soviet Union.

It was not until 1953 that my first-hand acquaintance with European affairs was renewed after the interruption of the war, and some experience in Asia was begun, when I left the government for work with the Ford Foundation in charge of its international affairs programs. One of our main hopes was to reduce the tension of a sharp conflict in Europe between East and West by reinstating some intellectual exchanges between the U.S. and the Soviet satellites. Poland and Yugoslavia seemed the most receptive. I was welcomed promptly into Poland in 1957 after its assertion of partial independence in 1956 and an exploratory visit by my colleague, Shepard Stone. The Poles, including even many of those still committed to communism, were eager to develop a measure of independence, and demonstrated a sometimes embarrassing freedom of opinion and invective against the Soviets in conversations over public luncheon tables. Such attitudes were especially intense in Cracow, where the university professors, no matter how secular their beliefs, were proud of the traditions of centuries of Polish leadership defending western Catholicism against the incursions of the Orthodox czars.

The scientists were particularly cynical about the pretensions of Marxism to scientific objectivity. A party bureaucrat took me to visit one of the country's most noted physicists, Leopold Infeld, a collaborator of Einstein's, who had been given a chateau as a residence by the Polish government. After some solemn discussion of the procedural problems of managing an international scholarly exchange, Infeld remarked that the Ford Foundation would of course have to take into account Khrushchev's recent visit to the Pope. When I showed my surprise, he went on (as my notes recorded) more or less like this:

"I'm not surprised you don't know about the visit; it was kept very quiet. Khrushchev was shown up the back stairs of the Vatican and after the polite preliminaries said, 'Holy Father, I need your advice.'

'Yes, Comrade Khrushchev, how can I help you?'

'Well, it's like this, Holy Father. We run the two biggest worldwide systems, you and I, and they are very similar indeed in many respects. But you somehow keep firm control of yours while I'm always in trouble. I bring my people in from the outlying dioceses, Poland, Rumania, and all the rest, and entertain them royally. We show them everything—our farms, our factories, our laboratories. And still they go home and are rebellious. What can I do about it? What can we learn from you?'

'Well, Comrade, I'm surprised that you have never noticed our fundamental operating principle, the one that keeps us out of such difficulties.'

'Yes, Holy Father, what is it?'

'Comrade, we never let our faithful see our Paradise.'"

My bureaucratic guide rushed me away—not, as I first assumed, in distaste for such heresy, but in order to tell the story to the rector of the Catholic University of Lublin.

With this kind of skepticism, the Poles were not receptive to the assertions of Marxist dogma. While I was in Warsaw the International Institute of Philosophy was having its Congress there, trying to bridge the differences in approach between East and West. I met on the street, quite by accident, a philosopher from the University of Chicago who was president of the institute and who got me admitted as an observer to some of its meetings. The high point in the proceedings, as far as I was concerned, was the speech by a delegate from the Peoples' Republic of China, who had himself been educated many years earlier at Columbia University. He reproached the Polish philosophers for their deviationism and asserted that the International Institute of Philosophy should recognize that the three greatest social scientists of the twentieth century were Lenin, Stalin, and Mao Tse-tung.

The Yugoslavs were temperamentally less open and receptive than the Poles. Indeed, I got into the country in May, 1958, with great difficulty after months of refusal to grant me a visa and then for several days found the Belgrade officials most uncommunicative. But then came a break. The Yugoslav Communist party congress in Ljubljana in April had taken a quite independent line from that of Moscow as it adopted its program, thus offending the Soviets. Then in May the Chinese Communist party congress had launched a violent attack on Tito and Yugoslav deviationism and especially on any Communist country's contacts with the United States. In response, the Yugoslav government apparently decided, just after my arrival in Belgrade, to defy the Chinese and Russian pressure and open up even more relations with the West.

All of this, of course, I learned only much later; so I was totally surprised when suddenly the atmosphere cleared, my negotiations began to prosper, and I found it easy to arrange a series of foundation-supported exchanges. Later I summoned up my courage to ask why they had been so suspicious of me earlier. The answer from a cultural affairs officer with whom I had worked up a friendship was explicit: because, in my efforts to get a visa, I had managed by telephone to locate the Yugoslav ambassador to the U.S., in Paris, where he was on a confidential visit, it seemed obvious that I was connected with the Central Intelligence Agency. As a matter of fact, the phone call was made from my hotel room in Bologna, and (since I had thought the ambassador in question was at the time in Belgrade) the credit for finding him in Paris should have gone entirely to the hotel phone operator.

Since Yugoslavia incorporated Slovenia, formerly Roman Catholic, with the Eastern Orthodox areas of Serbia and Bosnia and included areas that had been freed of Turkish rule only during the twentieth century, there were traces of the old religious conflicts that persisted more strongly in Poland. One church on the Danube had on its steeple both a cross and a crescent; I was told, and was almost gullible enough to believe, that it had changed hands between Christians and Moslems so often during the centuries of warfare that they were tired of changing the symbols. Then I was also told that the recent party congress in Ljubljana had been held in a church that had been deconsecrated for the purpose and then reconsecrated with a new title: the Church of the Sixth Party Congress. I began to wonder whether any country that had not first, on religious grounds, broken the connection between ecclesiastical and political authority could ever establish a free and pluralistic constitutional system.

As I traveled in Asia on foundation business, the earlier history of religious influence on politics impressed me. In the Near East, many of the revolutionary political leaders against the old Ottoman Empire and later against French and British domination had been educated at the Syrian Protestant College, later named the American University of Beirut, the products of Congregational missionary enterprise. Somewhat similar influence had apparently been exerted in China by the various missionary colleges. The situation in India and Pakistan was similarly confusing, as Gandhi's followers tried to make Hinduism, and Jinnah's followers to make Islam, the basis for new political systems. But as difficulties developed in such approaches the main reliance of the Indian subcontinent was on the civil service as the unifying force of the constitutional system. In this respect India was in far better shape than Indonesia or Viet Nam, where the Dutch and French had done little to develop competent native bureaucracies. It was even more fortunate than Pakistan, where the dominant social groups were more likely to go for military rather than civil service careers. As one weary Moslem governor of West Pakistan confided in me, he had little hope that the new effort to base political ideology on Islamic rather than Christian thought would be useful; after all, he said, "Islam is a political system of autocracy tempered by assassination."

In dollar amounts, the Ford Foundation's program of economic and political development in Asia was small potatoes compared to that of the U.S. government. But it had certain advantages; as an unofficial agency it could operate more flexibly and plan its activities over a longer period, unconstrained by the cycles of federal appropriations deadlines. But its time perspective was still far too short. The idea that to reduce poverty would automatically establish democracy seemed more and more illusory as it became plain that traditional religious beliefs and political attitudes were also fundamental obstacles.

Several years after leaving the foundation, I had a chance to observe the most severe conflict between old beliefs and the processes of modernization. It was an unusual experience: not many students of government have a chance to serve as a constitutional adviser to a king who is also a god.

The King of Nepal, as far as I know, is the only contemporary ruler whose subjects believe that he not only has a divine right to rule but is himself divine. That status did not keep the kings of the Hindu dynasty from being maintained as figureheads, virtually imprisoned in their palace, by the Rana maharajahs for more than a century until they were reestablished in actual power by a popular revolution in 1951. They then, in order to establish a modern basis for rule, asked the leading theorist of the British parliamentary system, Ivor Jennings, to write a constitution for them. A few years later King Mahendra, on a state visit to the United States, confided to President Eisenhower that he did not understand the constitution and wished that Eisenhower would send over someone to explain it to him. Since (as I will tell later) I was then serving on an advisory committee for the President, I was assigned that mission: while formally I undertook it as a Foreign Service Reserve Officer, it was essential in Katmandu that I be perceived as an independent adviser to the King, without any active connection with the United States Embassy, so I was given Nepalese staff help and a suite in the King's guest palace.

I soon found myself in an acute conflict of interest. The Prime Minister, B. P. Koirala, was supported by a party modeled on the Indian Congress party, a secular and modernizing party with an approach based more on economics and sociology than on Hindu theology. It might have served to support the King's professed hope to establish a constitutional monarchy with a parliamentary cabinet system. But following the example of the Indian Congress party, it made no secret of its ultimate intention of abolishing the monarchy.

The King consulted me on this issue and made it clear that he might therefore abolish the constitution and the Parliament; I gave him the inaccurate advice that his military forces, equipped with out-of-date Enfield rifles and a few pieces of rusty artillery, were inadequate to support a *coup d'etat*. I then took a plane to New York with the Prime Minister, on his way to attend a United Nations meeting, and tried to warn him that his public statements that the monarchy should ultimately be abolished involved obvious risks. My advice carried no weight in either direction. Later that autumn, at a time when the ambassadors to Nepal of most of the major powers were away, the King called out the troops, abolished the constitution and the parliament, and put the entire Cabinet into confinement.

I feared that some of my new friends among the ministers would be executed. But I had not understood the theological complexities of Hinduism: the King, while a god, was still not of the highest Hindu caste, the Brahmins. He was only a member of the second or warrior caste, the Kshatriyas. To shed the blood of a Brahmin would have been an unpardonable sin, and Prime Minister Koirala and several of his colleagues were Brahmins. They remained in protective custody, presumably in comfort, in a local palace until the King released them eight years later and exiled them to India.

I have given up any idea that I could really understand the interaction of political and religious ideas, but it does seem clear to me that a ruler or a ruling class cannot force freedom and self-government on a people unless their beliefs are compatible with it. But Robert Graves, in his novels *I, Claudius* and *Claudius the God*, suggested it many years ago.

1. In one letter to Thomas Law, June 13, 1814, and another to John Adams, April 8, 1816. See Adrienne Koch and William Peden (eds.), *The Life and Selected Writings of Thomas Jefferson* (New York, 1944), 636, 667.

2. Robert K. Merton, *The Sociology of Science* (Chicago, 1973), 190.

3. Peter Gay tells how Voltaire in his old age came to seem timid and traditional to all-out materialists like Holbach in *The Rise of Modern Paganism*, 397–99, vol. I of Gay, *The Enlightenment: An Interpretation* (New York, 1966).

4. A brief selection of materials from Comte's massive six-volume *Course of Positive Philosophy* (1830–42), outlining the basis of his social views, may be found in Stanislaw Andreski (ed.), *The Essential Comte* (New York, 1974). A longer selection by Comte himself from the six volumes, which he renamed the *System of Positive Philosophy*, was prepared in 1848 under the title, *A General View of Positivism* (rpr. New York, 1957).

5. Auguste Comte, *The Catechism of Positive Religion* (1858; rpr. Clifton, N.J., 1973), 2–5.

6. *Ibid.*, 52–54.

7. *Ibid.*, 238–41.

8. *Ibid.*, 8–9, 18–19, 222–26. The same points are made in his *General View of Positivism*, 263–67.

9. Gertrude Himmelfarb, "The Descent of the Huxleys," *Atlantic Monthly* (August, 1968), 90.

10. Donald Fleming's introduction to Jacques Loeb, *The Mechanistic Conception of Life* (Cambridge, Mass., 1964), describes the close connections between the advanced sciences and radical politics in late nineteenth century Germany.

11. Adam Ulam, *The Bolsheviks* (New York, 1965), esp. 54–59, 217–68.

12. "Westminster Confession of Faith," Chap. XVI, in John H. Leith (ed.), *Creeds of the Churches* (Richmond, 1973), 211.

13. Whitney R. Cross, *The Burned-Over District* (New York, 1965).

14. Leszek Kolakowski, formerly one of the most influential young Marxist philosophers at the University of Warsaw, was expelled from Poland in 1968 and became a senior fellow of All Souls College, Oxford, and a visiting professor at Montreal, Berkeley, Yale, and the University of Chicago. His major books include *Main Currents of Marxism* and *Marxism and Beyond*. The quotations here are from an interview he gave to George Urban, *Encounter* (January, 1981), 9–26, esp. 12, which undertakes to sum up the lessons to be learned from his longer works.

15. The issue has arisen most notably in the distinction affirmed by Jeane J. Kirkpatrick, U.S. ambassador to the United Nations, between traditional authoritarian and totalitarian regimes in the conduct of U.S. policy. This distinction, by which she defended the continued support of authoritarian regimes in Central America, had been developed in her *Dictatorships and Double Standards* (New York, 1982).

16. Simón Bolívar, "Memorial to the Citizens of New Granada by a Citizen of Caracas, Cartagena de Indias," Dec. 15, 1812, quoted by Gottfried Dietze, "Government of the People: A European Looks at the Americas," *Américas*, XXXIII (May, 1981), 10–12.

17. Reinhold Niebuhr, *The Nature and Destiny of Man* (New York, 1947), II, 131–34, argues that this perfectionist tendency in Eastern Orthodox thought is the result of the persistence of Hellenist philosophy, and its distortion of Hebraic ideas. In a somewhat similar way, Gerhard B. Ladner contrasts the thought of Saint Augustine with that of several Orthodox fathers and argues that the Eastern Orthodox belief in perfectibility led to giving more preference to the monastic and less to the secular orders than was true in the Roman church, thus making the Eastern church less interested in social reform. See Gerhard B. Ladner, *The Idea of Reform* (Cambridge, Mass., 1959), esp. 190–99.

18. Andreski (ed.), *The Essential Comte*, 168.

19. Herbert Spencer, *Social Statics* (New York, 1865), 78, 80, 93.

20. Herbert Spencer, *Study of Sociology*, 1873, excerpted in J. D. Y. Peel (ed.), *Herbert Spencer and Social Evolution* (Chicago, 1972), 110.

21. Herbert Spencer, *Principles of Sociology*, 1876, excerpted *ibid.*, 190–99.

22. Robert Green McCloskey (ed.), *Works of James Wilson* (Cambridge, Mass., 1967), I, 77–81.

Chapter IV. The Seamy Side of Sovereignty

On returning from Oxford during the depths of the Depression in 1935, I was more clear about what I was interested in than about how I could earn a living at it. A couple of years later, after several changes in Washington jobs and then living out of a suitcase for a year while studying city governments across the country, I wrote in a class letter to the *American Oxonian* that "my hope for a permanent career is to continue working on the point where politics meets administration, and I don't care whether the job is journalistic, bureaucratic, academic, or erratic, just so it isn't peripatetic."

I had these various jobs because, while my first inclination had been journalism, I could find no newspaper job to my taste. Hoping for one on the Washington *Post*, I took the advice of its editor, Felix Morley, and got a government job at $1,800 a year to support myself while writing occasional feature articles for him on the side. But with my lack of success as a journalist I blundered into a series of administrative and research jobs that provided the ideal experience for one who needed to appreciate more clearly the ways in which American practice differed from British theory.

These experiences started with a role in an effort to use something like the British committee approach to interdepartmental coordination. They then included several chances to observe the ways in which policy and administration intersect in both local and federal governments. And finally they included immersion in the way science affects American politics—one of the most important elements in limiting executive authority and establishing the political autonomy of administrative agencies.

I was first hired by the Home Owners' Loan Corporation (HOLC), which had taken out mortgages on one-sixth of all urban homes in America in order to save from bankruptcy not only their owners and the home finance and building industries but also most of the local governments, with their heavy reliance on real property taxes. The HOLC Chairman was also running the Federal Home Loan Bank Board (FHLBB), founded during the Hoover administration as a credit reserve for building and loan associations. But a few months later I was asked to serve as personal assistant to the chairman of a new system of coordination for government agencies in the housing field, the Central Housing Committee. The chairman was FDR's uncle, Frederic A. Delano, who had been given the impossible task of trying to reconcile the programs of eight major agencies, ranging from the fiscally conservative Farm Credit Administration and Federal Home Loan Banks to Rexford Tugwell's Resettlement Administration and the Public Housing Division of the Public Works Administration, staffed by eager young radicals whose models were the socialist housing projects of Central Europe.

The experience was a perfect antidote to one who had been overimpressed by the British system of coordinating committees. We had a general committee with an elaborate system of eight functional subcommittees, and in all of them the members came to meetings not prepared to negotiate out their differences but resolved to resist any change that would upset their backers outside the administration—not only the congressional committees but also the sources of their competitive support, such as municipal officers, mortgage bankers, lumber dealers, trade associations, labor unions, and other interests that had free access to the substance of our deliberations and that were intent on defending their special points of view by political action. When some years later, a unified housing agency (later named the Department of Housing and Urban Development) was created, it was impossible to contain all these diverse interests under a single roof, and the mortgage credit reserve boards (serving farm credit and the home loan banks) demanded to be left out.

The demands of this job on my time were highly irregular, leaving me leisure not only to study the history of housing and town planning in both the U.S. and Britain (with the help of visiting consultants to Delano such as Sir Raymond Unwin, who had helped develop the garden cities in England) but also to continue to nurse my hopes for a newspaper job. The editor of the Washington *Post*, knowing of my work at Oxford, recommended me to the publisher's wife, Agnes (Mrs. Eugene) Meyer, who was interested enough in civil service reform to forgive me for working for the people who were corrupting the FHLBB, which her husband had headed under Hoover. At her invitation in 1936 I wrote, out of my Oxford thesis, a series of articles on the British civil service which had a decisive influence on my later career. For they attracted the attention of Louis Brownlow, for whom I worked in one capacity or another, directly or indirectly, for more than a decade, and from whom I learned a great deal about the theory as well as the practice of American government.

His theory had been self-taught: as a sickly child in a Missouri village, he was expected to die soon and hence not sent to school at all. He learned to read by working around the village printing shop, and then became a newspaper reporter, a foreign correspondent, a commissioner (under Woodrow Wilson) of the District of Columbia, and later a city manager. He had become an influential adviser to the Rockefeller philanthropies on their programs in public health, and later in teamwork with Charles E. Merriam, a founder of the Social Science Research Council, he set up a new corporate entity (the Public Administration Clearing House—PACH) to bring together into a common headquarters at 1313 East 60th Street, near the University of Chicago, a group of national associations of public agencies and government officials, such as the Council of State Governments, the associations of governors, mayors, personnel and finance officers, and Brownlow's favorite outfit, the International City Managers' Association.

A half century before political scientists found it fashionable to discuss mediating institutions and the role of community organizations in national affairs, the group of independent associations that Brownlow gathered together began to play an influential role in the New Deal programs. Those programs relied heavily on federal grants to state and local governments in such fields as welfare and social security, housing, transportation, agriculture, and economic development. Not only were the states and cities important as agents of federal policy, but their lobbying influence insured that their point of view had to be taken into account as policies and programs developed. A majority of these associations have now moved their headquarters offices to Washington and built up substantial staffs, heavily supported either by federal research contracts or indirectly as overhead on federal program grants.

Two general points came out clearly in what I saw of Brownlow's operations and in the work I did for him. First, the fields of policy and of administration cannot be neatly separated, and the career officer must play a responsible role in both on a nonpolitical or at least nonpartisan basis. Second, the improvement of the career service must depend heavily on the professional motivation of the career officers themselves and may sometimes be handicapped as well as helped by the reform efforts of well-meaning private citizens or by the legalistic protection of city charters or judicial review.

The first job for which Brownlow recruited me was to be the co-author of a study of the city manager form of local government. It was supported by the Committee on Public Administration (which Brownlow chaired) of the Social Science Research Council, and I was teamed up with a far more experienced researcher and administrator, Harold A. Stone, and his wife Kathryn. The orthodox academic interpretation of the role of the city manager had been stated in his book on the subject by Leonard D. White, who saw the manager as America's most promising illustration of the need to separate management cleanly from policy interests in the interest of economy and efficiency.

As we went to twenty cities over a two-year period and read reports on other cities by volunteer collaborators, it began to seem clear to me that the ideal of nonpartisan service could not be advanced by ruling the managers out of any policy influence: policy grew out of administrative necessity, and American politicians would never concede to managers the confidential status necessary to protect their managerial role or support their freedom from patronage and corruption, unless the public could see that they were leading the community toward desirable program objectives. It made no sense to impose on them constraints that would have crippled the work of public health officers, agricultural county agents, or superintendents of schools.

Brownlow was tactically at odds with the principal private citizens' organization dedicated to the improvement of local government, the National Municipal League. The league had not originally supported the city manager plan, which had been invented by a young journalist, Richard S. Childs, and pushed by the National Short Ballot Organization, which Woodrow Wilson headed. Wilson had distrusted the league, having more faith than its leaders in politicians and clearcut systems of political responsibility. But the league became the city manager plan's most conspicuous backer. As it did so, it defined its theory in the model charter for cities, which undertook to spell out in legalistic detail the respective authority of the city council and the city manager, thus (as Brownlow saw the issue and as our surveys led me to believe) converting the plan from one of unification of powers in the council to a separation of powers between it and the manager. But a separation of powers is not very useful if one power's tenure depends on the discretion of the other, especially if the other is a council elected, as the model charter proposed, by a system of proportional representation which would make a coherent majority difficult to maintain.

After our studies of city manager government were completed and published, I went to work for the Public Administration Clearing House, formally as editor of its news bulletins and publications, but more generally doing staff work of all kinds for Brownlow, including his futile efforts to influence the revisions of the model charter. His disagreement with the National Municipal League leaders, and with Leonard White, was not profound enough to destroy his friendship or alliance with them since they were all dedicated to generally the same ends. But he was clearly less interested in the traditional legalistic approach to administration, more interested in actual participation in government than in the approach of moral reform, and eager to encourage the technical and professional competence of specialists actively engaged in general program development.

My recurrent interest in British politics led me, just before leaving Chicago for military service, to write an article for *Public Administration Review,* "The Parliamentary and Presidential Systems." Especially in that new and obscure journal, it would never have attracted attention but for the fact that Harold Laski, who must have had it called to his attention, chose to write a rebuttal to it. I was astonished, because my criticism of parliamentary government was nothing like as severe as he had often expressed; indeed, I had deliberately avoided listing him among my sources, thinking that it would be more persuasive to cite conservative authorities for my radical argument. This mild controversy seemed to attract more scholarly attention than I had expected; the articles were used after the war as required reading for freshmen in Harvard's introductory course in government and may have had some influence in leading to my invitation years later to join that faculty as a political scientist.

While I had felt some obligation to work as a civilian on the war effort of the organizations of state and local governments, I was obsessed after Pearl Harbor by the compulsion to get into military service. The navy commissioned me but, finding that I was thirty pounds underweight by its standards, refused to put me on unrestricted or combat service and had some trouble finding me an assignment. In order to get on active duty, I found an opportunity to get myself transferred to the coast guard as a lieutenant, junior grade. But the personnel system of the coast guard put me into a headquarters administrative job which had no combat glamor but brought me more closely in touch with two fundamental aspects of federal administration.

The first was the influence of science. The coast guard had inherited the oldest federal regulatory program, the Steamboat Inspection Service. It had been founded on the initiative of a private scientific institution, the Franklin Institute of Philadelphia, which had been given a contract to study a narrow technical subject: what caused steamboat boilers to blow up? With the scientists' typical disregard for administrative constraints, the study went on from its technical question to recommend that the federal government establish the first regulatory program. All of this I had to explore when assigned the job of helping the coast guard work out anew the relation between its military task for the navy—such as landings on the South Pacific beaches—and its regular responsibilities for insuring the safety of shipping and the security of domestic ports.

The second aspect of federal administration was the degree of independence of agencies whose programs were founded on scientific skills and jealously guarded by the guilds of scientific professionals, inside or outside the government service. The coast guard was a splendid illustration; it should have been, by administrative theory, completely subordinate to the navy's hierarchical command structure, under which it was placed in wartime. But with the support of shipping interests and maritime unions and congressional subcommittees, it set a spectacular example—as far as top-level organizational issues went—of patriotic insubordination.

The same two issues came up later in a series of assignments for which the director of the Budget Bureau, Harold D. Smith, borrowed me from the coast guard. I was put to work studying for the bureau the state governments' system of civil defense, a study which took me to Tennessee, where I found that neither the governor nor I could find out how the security arrangements were organized at Oak Ridge. My father, a railroad man, had told me of his wonderment at hauling many tons of raw material in to Oak Ridge but having no ammunition to haul out. Then I helped the bureau explore the proposal for a postwar system of universal military training, including training in civilian public service jobs, which was being pushed by the unlikely alliance of General Marshall's old mentor, General John McAuley Palmer, and Eleanor Roosevelt. But finally and most significant, I was put to work for the bureau on a study of the Office of Scientific Research and Development and had to try to understand the intricacies of a system of contractual relations by which private educational institutions were charged with developing the most sophisticated new weapons of World War II. Here the combination of scientific professionalism and private institutional status completely defeated the channels of command of the military hierarchy.

While I was fully licensed to look at the work on radar, guided missiles, and the other novelties of the OSRD program, I was of course denied any access to the atomic energy program. All I knew—and I only dimly suspected a connection with the Oak Ridge mystery—was that most of the leading theoretical physicists of the country, unlike the top scientists of other disciplines who were engaged on other weapons programs, had disappeared. The mystery was cleared up in August, 1945, when news came of the Hiroshima bomb. Harold Smith, who had already asked me to study for him the future plans of the federal government for the support of basic science through a national science foundation, doubled my troubles by asking me to look also at the proposals for an atomic energy agency. The basic problem in both cases turned on the extent to which scientific knowledge (especially when scientists were hired as private citizens under a contractual system rather than as government career officers) should be used to justify a degree of independence from political authority. The leading scientists from the OSRD were advocating that both agencies (the future National Science Foundation and Atomic Energy Commission) should be headed by boards of private citizens, serving the government on a part-time basis and presumably to be drawn from leading scientific institutions, rather than by full-time officers appointed by the President. With respect to both agencies, I shared the Budget Bureau's view in giving more weight to hierarchical responsibility than to scientific independence. But the problem was too complex to be solved easily by any rigid principle, and it was fascinating enough to lead me to make it my main research concern; since I later produced two books on the subject, I need not go into more detail here.

For one obsessed with the question of the proper role and scope of administration in government, it seemed clear that the dynamic new role of science had changed everything. When I was released from military service I continued to serve the Budget Bureau as a civilian, for a time as head of its Government Organization Branch. In that job, which carried responsibility for staff work on the President's reorganization plans, it seemed clear to me that the purpose of administrative organization was no longer economy and efficiency, as it had been in a static era, but had become the protection of the President's constitutional function, including the guarantee of procedures by which the Congress could hold him truly accountable for general policy as well as detailed procedural regularity.

For several years I oscillated between the staff of the Budget Bureau and my old employer, the Public Administration Clearing House, which made me the head of its Washington office. In that capacity I was employed under contract—the administrative types had indeed learned some procedural lessons from the OSRD scientists—to work with the Hoover Commission on a study of the presidency, which may more appropriately be discussed in the next chapter's notes.

But in the meantime I continued my part-time interest in the work of the scientists and their relation to military issues. In part, this was as a consultant to the Budget Bureau. But more and more my work was in direct relationship to the military services, through their elaborate system of part-time civilian advisory committees. I was made a member of the Subpanel on Scientific and Specialized Personnel of the Panel on Human Behavior of the Committee on Human Resources of the Research and Development Board of the National Military Establishment. This esoteric group of social scientists was concerned with the future system of mobilization of science for military research. It had a very difficult time sorting out its concern for scientific freedom from the need for military secrecy. When the military began to worry more about Communist spies, the security officers began to demand that we as consultants keep our committee notes in safes that met military requirements, which they would supply at government expense. When my secretary asked why my safe had not been delivered to my office, she was told that such equipment could not be supplied until all the formalities of my appointment had been completed, including my security clearance. She then asked what I should do with the restricted documents I already had. The security officer answered, "Until Mr. Price has been proved loyal to the United States, he will have to keep his classified documents in an open file."

I thought this funny enough to report in a lecture a few weeks later at West Point. Some of the faculty there solemnly debated what I should do, and unanimously advised me that it was my duty to write the story up and submit it to the *New Yorker*. Which I did, disguising the names of the panels and committees slightly, and the *New Yorker* included it in its "Talk of the Town" and paid me ten dollars; I have often wondered what government regulations I violated by accepting the fee.

The security issue, however, was a genuine one, and when James A. Perkins became deputy chairman of the Research and Development Board (RDB) at the Pentagon he asked me to chair a committee to review its security procedures and the cases that arose within them. It soon became clear to me, during the panic that was caused in the civil service by Senator Joe McCarthy's investigations, that certain members of the RDB staff were feeding tips to the senator's staff and that there was nothing we could do about it. It was also clear that in our security committee I could not rely on civilian staff for balanced judgments on their colleagues, since they themselves felt too vulnerable, while career military officers could be fairer in evaluating minor political indiscretions on the part of scientists who were naïve in such matters. They, as career military officers, were above suspicion themselves and inclined to think that it was only normal for scientists to be slightly nutty.

Lest the reader think that I am exaggerating the hysterical pressures of the era, I may recall that our committee had to deal with charges brought against one very eminent scientist on the grounds that his wife had been teaching in a Unitarian Sunday school.

But the issue was real enough. I continued my responsibility for RDB security matters when James Perkins left the deputy chairman's job and I took his place. In this capacity I became aware of the fact that the chairman of the board's Atomic Energy Committee, J. Robert Oppenheimer, had been subject to some suspicion on grounds of security, but that the issue had been settled for the time being at higher levels, and I would do well to ignore it. When it blew into the open a few years later, and became the basis for an elaborate legalistic procedure that led to public withdrawal of Oppenheimer's security clearances even though the prosecution acknowledged that he had done nothing wrong himself, I wondered more and more about the utility of such formalized procedures and of freedom of information in such cases. Some years later I asked Lord Bridges, the top civil servant in Great Britain, how the U.K. would have handled such a case. The answer was that by discretionary authority the proper officers would have withdrawn security clearance without having to explain why, without informing the Parliament, and without making a public issue of the matter or blackening the scientist's reputation. (Indeed, the Personnel Security Board for the U.S. Atomic Energy Commission reported that it would have proposed a similar course of action "if we were allowed to exercise mature practical judgment without the rigid circumspection of regulations and criteria established for us.") The United Kingdom's record on security issues has been by no means perfect, but with respect to the protection of individual freedom, it leads one to wonder whether it is better to rely on publicity or discretionary authority.

The Research and Development Board was a part of a system designed to give the several military services a chance to participate in and veto the policies of the Department of Defense. It was a classic example of the ways in which interdepartmental committees can frustrate responsible policy. When after Eisenhower's election his advisers on organization, chaired by Nelson A. Rockefeller, proposed a study of the Defense Department, they asked me to be the staff director of the study. My frustration in the board had taught me to be skeptical of the effectiveness of political authority. I said I would be glad to try it but thought that one condition was essential for success. A reorganization proposal to reduce the particularism of the services and increase the responsibility of the secretary of defense could succeed only if the entire operation could be completed in six weeks; a longer study would give the navy time to bring the admirals in from sea duty and set them to lobbying with congressional committees. So it was planned: the secretary of defense set up the Committee on the Organization of the Department of Defense on February 19, 1953, and the committee completed its work on the report on April 4.

While I was wholeheartedly in favor of more effective unification of the services, and against the navy's desire to maintain its independence, I could not avoid a sneaking admiration for its professional spirit. The army, with all its Corps of Engineers work on rivers and harbors and other civilian operations and with its large proportion of officers drawn from the national guard, was much more attuned to domestic politics. The navy carried its professional pride as a floating empire of its own to an unreasonable degree, and I was highly critical of its disregard, verging on contempt, for civilian politics.

But one incident made me modify my attitude a trifle. Shortly after Eisenhower's election, the RDB Chairman (Walter G. Whitman) and I were being flown in a navy plane to land on an aircraft carrier that was testing some new weapons system at sea off Cape Hatteras. In rough and cloudy weather, the navy lieutenant who was at the controls had trouble finding the carrier and while cruising in search of it he turned on a commercial radio news program and we heard the announcement that Eisenhower was to appoint Charles E. Wilson, of General Motors fame, as secretary of defense. While we were exclaiming our surprise, the lieutenant expressed mild interest and then added, "By the way, who is secretary of defense now?"

I was outraged by this evidence that a career navy officer had not been interested enough in the broad governmental picture even to bother to learn who was his civilian superior. But then came a break in the clouds and far below—it seemed miles below—we could see the carrier on which we were to land. It looked about as big as a teacup, bouncing on the waves. And all of a sudden I did not want that navy pilot to have the slightest concern with the policies or the identity of his political superiors: I only wanted him to know how to land that plane. Which he did. And ever since, although I have not given up my conviction that a career government official should be interested in a broader range of issues than his own bureau, I have been forced grudgingly to admit that some narrowness of vision is inevitable in a career system.

As a result of the report of the Rockefeller Committee, the RDB was abolished and my job with it. One of the by-products of the committee's report was the proposal to give some coherence to the joint research efforts of the several services through the Weapons Systems Evaluation Group, which had been staffed by career military and civil service officers, and had been too deeply torn by service rivalries to be effective. The committee recommended imitating the experience of the Rand Corporation, through which the air force had provided first-rate work on a contractual basis. The Institute for Defense Analyses was accordingly incorporated for the purpose and (like Rand) given some nominal independence with a grant of funds from the Ford Foundation—this after I had left government and gone on that foundation's staff. But the outcome simply demonstrated that independent funding was not enough to bridge the policy differences high in the governmental hierarchy. What Rand could do on comparatively technical issues for the air force, it could not do for the issues at the level of the secretary of defense and the presidency, and these difficulties were compounded in the policy issues the Institute for Defense Analyses was set up to study. Which brings us to the problems of the presidency in the next chapter.

1. *New Statesman*, January 25, 1963, and London *Times*, January 24, 1963, p. 3.
2. A. E. Dick Howard, "A Litigation Society," *American Oxonian* (Fall, 1981), rpr. from *Wilson Quarterly*, V (Summer, 1981).
3. Frederick C. Mosher, *Democracy and the Public Service* (New York, 1968), Chap. III.
4. Otto L. Nelson, Jr., *National Security and the General Staff* (Washington, D.C., 1946), 292–95. See also John McAuley Palmer, *America in Arms* (New Haven, 1941).

5. G. Calvin Mackenzie, "The Paradox of Presidential Personnel Management," in Hugh Heclo and Lester M. Salamon (eds.), *The Illusion of Presidential Government* (Boulder, Colo., 1981), 113–46.

6. *The Civil Service: Report of the Committee* (Cmnd. 3638, 1968), vol. I. For a criticism of the failure of the government to effect the report recommendations in full, see Peter Kellner and Lord Crowther-Hunt, *The Civil Servants* (London, 1980).

7. Frederick C. Mosher, "The Changing Responsibilities and Tactics of the Federal Government" (draft paper prepared for the National Academy of Public Administration, Washington, D.C., 1980).

8. Robert Presthus, "Mrs. Thatcher Stalks the Quango: A Note on Patronage and Justice in Britain," *Public Administration Review*, XLI (May-June, 1981), 312–17.

9. Royal Commission on the Civil Service, 1929–30, Report (Cmd. 3909, 1930), Appendix VIII, 5–7.

10. President's Committee on Administrative Management, *Administrative Management in the Government of the United States* (Washington, D.C., 1937), 7–8; Commission on Organization of the Executive Branch of the Government, *Task Force Report on Personnel and Civil Service* (Washington, D.C., 1955), 7, 8; Commission on Organization of the Executive Branch of the Government, *Personnel and Civil Service: A Report to the Congress* (Washington, D.C., 1955).

11. Standing Order of the House of Commons, December 11, 1706. Sir Thomas Erskine May, *Constitutional History of England* (New York, 1882), I, 443. The current status of this rule is explained in Sir Barnett Cocks (ed.), *Erskine May's Treatise on the Law, Privileges, Proceedings, and Usage of Parliament* (18th ed.; London, 1971), Chap. XXVII.

12. Treasury Circular, March 12, 1920, in *Epitome of the Reports from the Committees of Public Accounts, 1875–1925* (HC 161, 1927), 1271–72.

13. Leonard D. White, *The Jeffersonians* (New York, 1951), 109.

14. Leonard D. White, *The Republican Era, 1869–1901* (New York, 1958), 65.

15. Arthur Smithies, *The Budgetary Process in the United States* (New York, 1955), Chap. IV. The story of the study of the British system and its imitation by the U.S. is told by W. F. Willoughby, a member of the Taft Commission, and director of the Institute for Government Research (later part of the Brookings Institution) in his *National Budget System* (Baltimore, 1927), esp. Chap. II. For a more recent account of the budgetary process and its decline in influence, see Allen Schick, "The Problem of Presidential Budgeting," in Heclo and Salamon (eds.), *Illusion of Presidential Government*, 85–112.

16. John Adams, to Roger Sherman, n.d., in Charles Francis Adams (ed.), *The Works of John Adams* (Boston, 1850–56), VI, 432.

17. Louis Brownlow, *A Passion for Anonymity* (Chicago, 1958), Chap. 29.

18. *Ibid.*, 414.

19. Tam Dalyell, "Cabinetmaking," *New Scientist*, June 14, 1979, p. 937. For an earlier statement on this issue, see Herbert Morrison in *Parliamentary Debates*, House of Commons (Hansard) February 28, 1946, Columns 2129–32. Morrison at that time made it clear that the Cabinet felt it should not even admit the existence of its committees.

20. Samuel H. Beer, *Britain Against Itself: The Political Contradictions of Collectivism* (New York, 1982), 168–69.

21. Prime Minister Thatcher's statement on the abolition of the Civil Service Department and the transfer of those of its responsibilities dealing with the promotion of top civil servants to the secretary of the Cabinet was made to the House of Commons on November 11, 1981. See her statement in *Hansard* for November 12, 1981, or the report in *Economist*, November 14, 1981, p. 63.

22. Eric Deakins, a former minister, in Manchester *Guardian*, June 26, 1979, p. 10. See also Richard H. S. Crossman, *The Myths of Cabinet Government* (Cambridge, Mass., 1972). For examples from Crossman's *The Diaries of a Cabinet Minister* (New York, 1977), see I, 90, 200, 343, 614–16. See also comments on Crossman's *Diaries* in Lord Hailsham, *The Dilemma of Democracy* (London, 1978), 207.

23. For a typical incident illustrating the normal practice, see Crossman, *Diaries of a Cabinet Minister*, II, 343–44. The issue over the Falklands inquiry is described in the London newspapers in early July, 1982, especially in the *Daily Telegraph* of July 2 ("Heath Attacks Thatcher," 1) and in the London *Times* of July 9, with its full quotation of Prime Minister Thatcher's statement in the House of Commons on July 8.

24. Bill C-43, An Act to Enact the Access to Information Act and the Privacy Act, etc., as passed by the Canadian House of Commons, June 28, 1982, Schedule III, Section 36.

25. Lawrence C. Dodd and Richard L. Schott, *Congress and the Administrative State* (New York, 1979), Chap. 4, pp. 106–54; Michael Malbin, *Unelected Representatives* (New York, 1980), Chap. 10, pp. 239–51, and appendix, pp. 252–53.

26. Personal communication from Jack Watson, secretary of the cabinet under President Carter.

27. Laurence E. Lynn, Jr., *Managing the Public's Business* (New York, 1981), 17–20.

28. Louis Fisher, *The Constitution Between Friends* (New York, 1978).

29. *Hearings before the Subcommittee on the Separation of Powers of the Committee on the Judiciary*, U.S. Senate, 90th Cong., 1st Sess., 1967. For a discussion of the relation between congressional intervention and administrative abuses, see Louis Fisher, "Congress and the President in the Administrative Process: The Uneasy Alliance," in Heclo and Salamon (eds.), *Illusion of Presidential Government*, 35–40.

30. John C. Calhoun, *A Disquisition on Government* (New York, 1853), 105–106. Acton, in an 1861 essay, quoted Calhoun at great length and with high approval: *Essays on Church and State* (London, 1952), Chap. XI, 315–19.

Chapter V. The Institutional Presidency and the Cabinet

When the first Hoover Commission undertook its work on the organization of the government, I had the ideal vantage point—though at times one of some discomfort—for studying the presidency. I was assistant to former President Hoover for that study, designated for that purpose by President Truman at Hoover's request, and still on the payroll of the institution founded by President Roosevelt's principal adviser on government organization, Louis Brownlow. At the same time, I was assigned by Hoover to serve as the liaison between his commission and the expected beneficiary of its reforms—the heir apparent to the presidency, Thomas E. Dewey. I was to work with Governor Dewey's counsel (Charles D. Breitel, later a New York Supreme Court judge) to help plan how the Hoover Commission recommendations were to simplify Dewey's job as President.

But I am getting ahead of my story. It started, for this purpose, as noted in the previous chapter's reminiscences, when I finished my work on the study of the city manager plan of municipal government for the Social Science Research Council, and Louis Brownlow asked me to stay on in Chicago with his Public Administration Clearing House. The most interesting part of that work,though it would have never been acknowledged in a job description or an organization chart (Brownlow would never have permitted either in his outfit) was to help him on the follow-up on the reorganization plans that had been effected in 1939 as the result of the Brownlow Committee's report in 1937. The most important plan had created the Executive Office of the President, and in it was the Bureau of the Budget, with a new Division of Administrative Management, where the key positions were filled by Brownlow protégés.

That organization had been so successful in working on problems of organization and management that Brownlow's personal role as a presidential adviser was, on those particular subjects, much less needed by FDR, especially as the war preoccupied his attention. But on the higher aspect of administration—the level where it became mixed with constitutional issues—Roosevelt still occasionally sought his advice or was willing to consider it, as when they had agreed earlier that the mobilization plan (the M-Day Plan) proposed by the military would formalize advice to the President to such an extent that it would greatly inhibit his political discretion.

As the war wore on, and people began to worry about the postwar structure of government, Brownlow began to be fearful that Congress, being dissatisfied with Roosevelt's disorderly administrative habits, would legislate a high level of coordination in such rigid terms that it would be to the President's disadvantage. At the same time, he was convinced that the staff work in the Executive Office that he had helped to establish could never take care of high policy issues without greater participation on a more systematic basis by the responsible heads of departments—in short, without something more like a cabinet committee system.

I had been prepared to help him think about such issues by my studies of British government and my Washington experience with interdepartmental committees (see notes to Chapters II and IV). Accordingly, after long discussions, I took to my typewriter and drafted the document for Brownlow to send to the President. In it Brownlow recommended, with careful warnings against letting Congress set up by statute a system that would cramp the President's style, a postwar system by which the cabinet would be organized into committees covering the main fields of policy. Mechanically, the paper was turned out on my typewriter, but in substance every aspect of it was in accord with his instructions. If I made a contribution to it, it was not in the ghost-writing, but in the preliminary discussions which helped him translate his keen understanding of American politics into the terms that students of comparative constitutional systems were beginning to use.

The substance of the recommendations was, of course, less important than the tactic of getting them to the President's attention. He could not use the Budget Bureau; his old friends and protégés there had other wartime priorities and other ideas. He thought of the National Resources Planning

Board, but its staff director was sure to be unsympathetic. So he persuaded his old colleague Charles E. Merriam, one of the board's three members, to persuade the other two to present his paper unchanged to the President for his confidential consideration. Since the chairman of the board, Frederic A. Delano, was the President's uncle, he could convey it outside of official channels. Roosevelt replied to his uncle that he had read the paper but that he did not believe that Brownlow had the answer—or that anyone else did. And he added, "I am a bumblebee. I am going to keep on bumbling."

I came back to the problem of the cabinet and committee system three years later, after military service in U.S. coast guard headquarters, from which the Budget Bureau borrowed me for staff jobs on the several subjects noted in the preceding chapter notes. After getting out of uniform, I stayed on as a civilian in the Bureau of the Budget, for a time as acting head of the Government Organization Branch. There one of my preoccupations was in advising the director of the budget how to deal with the wide variety of proposals for a statutory system of cabinet councils or a cabinet secretariat. In 1946 Herbert Emmerich, Brownlow's successor at the Public Administration Clearing House, invited me to return there, but as head of its Washington office, one block north of the Executive Office building. In that position I could have greater freedom of personal choice but still collaborate with my old budget colleagues.

My choice was to worry about the many proposals for formalizing some aspect or another of a cabinet system. After discussion with the new budget director, James E. Webb, I addressed to him a memorandum entitled "Presidential or Cabinet Secretariat" that was intended for President Truman. It warned against a rigid statutory cabinet committee or secretariat system but urged that a new system be established under the President's discretionary control for involving cabinet members in confidential consultation on major policy issues.

A year or so later, when Mr. Webb proposed that I be designated by President Truman as their channel of communication to Hoover and his commission, I was sent to the President to be looked over. The President, unlike his predecessor, was a tidy and systematic person but one who liked to keep track of his most important problems and relationships himself, rather than relying completely on his staff. On his desk was a stack of leather folders in which he kept his notes on his major staff assignments. From the bottom of this small stack he pulled out the copy of my memorandum to Webb, which he said he had been reviewing from time to time as issues arose. I had considered it so confidential that I did not even keep a copy myself; I had to write to President Truman many years later to get one.

Hoover received me in his hotel suite for a polite and businesslike discussion. I felt obliged to start by confessing that I was by heredity and inclination a Democrat. That did not seem to worry him. Indeed, as I worked for him rather closely over the next year, I was surprised that it worried him so little. When I was alone with him he would often take telephone calls on intimate details of Republican party politics which I was embarrassed to overhear, but whenever I offered to leave the room so as to respect his privacy, he would always refuse. He was too formal and formidable a personality for me ever to feel relaxed as his aide, but I came to have high respect for his character and integrity and never shared the personal annoyance at him that was felt by some of the staff aides to the Democratic members of the commission.

He evidently had enough confidence in me to use my assistance. Years later, I found out through New York foundation circles that he had not relied entirely on his intuition but had had me checked out by the investigative staff of a major banking system. But his confidence in me personally, by which I was deeply gratified, did not extend to any willingness to use me as a ghost writer for his report. I prepared various drafts, all of which were too theoretical and academic in tone for his taste. He rejected them all and drafted the report, *The General Management of the Executive Branch*, himself in longhand on a yellow pad, saying that he wanted it short and simple enough so that the New York *Times* would publish it in full. Which it did.

Before then, two issues had been most contentious: the issue of the proper location of the executive budget staff and the issue of the proposal for a cabinet secretariat.

On the budget issues, Mr. Hoover was tempted for a while by various ideas that would lead either to having some sort of managerial deputy established by law under the President or to having the budget work set up in a strengthened Treasury Department rather than attached so directly to the President himself. It seemed to me essential to maintain the original idea of those who saw in 1919 and 1920 that, regardless of nominal location in the Treasury, the relationship to the President was all important: acts of Congress could alter the duties and authority of department secretaries but not—in basic Constitutional terms—the President's.

On this issue, I asked Hoover's permission to consult General Charles G. Dawes, who had been the first budget director, and later vice-president. I had easy personal access to him since he was an active and interested trustee of the Public Administration Clearing House. In spite of his later eminence as a Chicago banker, it was always clear that the Budget Bureau job had been his dearest experience. He had been chosen for it because of his fame as the general who was finance officer for General Pershing's American Expeditionary Forces in France during World War I. And that job may have been given him because, years before he became an eminent banker, he had been a member in a small Nebraska town of a chamber music trio; the other two were a young biologist named Roscoe Pound, who was soon to switch professions and later become dean of the Harvard Law School, and a young army lieutenant, John J. Pershing.

General Dawes (the military title was his favorite: he was never called

Ambassador Dawes in later life, or Vice-President Dawes) was clear that the budget office had to be attached to the President as a part of the President's Constitutional function, without direct statutory power of its own. He had refused President Harding's original offer of a cabinet position as secretary of the treasury, saying that the nominally subordinate job of budget director was far more important.

When I went to General Dawes with the issues, his response was prompt and explosive. After he moderated his reaction and put it in writing in more diplomatic terms, suitable for delivery to a former president, I conveyed it to Hoover. Whether its logic was persuasive, or Hoover saw the difficulty of moving against a powerful midwestern conservative, I neither knew nor cared. But the issue of an administrative vice-president was forgotten as far as the commission report was concerned, although Hoover continued to play with the idea later on.

In the second echelon of arguments the idea of putting the budget function back in the Treasury, with the treasury secretary in effective control (as he had not been from 1921 to 1939), continued to be debated. There was indeed a study group on accounting and auditing run by a very eminent accountant, formerly a member of the staff of the General Accounting Office, who was more interested in frugality and regularity than in the protection of the role of the President. I felt some discomfort in arguing with him on account of his eminence in the world of finance. But when, perhaps in an effort to be generous to my point of view, he said that he would not insist on having the proposed powers of the treasury secretary spelled out—like those of other department secretaries—in the Constitution but leave this flexible by defining them only by statute, I lost my awe for his political sophistication.

General Dawes, for all of his distaste for New Deal policies, never gave up his conviction that the American government needed a stronger presidency. As ambassador to Great Britain, he argued with the British Treasury that their committee-style coordination of policy was inferior to the businesslike management improvement efforts of the Budget Bureau. On this issue, I never dared express to him my disagreement.

He enjoyed telling me his views and reminiscing about them. On one such issue he was especially vehement, and this brings me to the second topic—the cabinet and its procedures. When I mentioned this issue, he went back to his old files. President-elect Coolidge had asked him, as vice-president-elect, to sit regularly in cabinet meetings. The general showed me his letter declining the invitation on principle. The principle was that no one should ever attend a cabinet meeting whose status would make it difficult for the President to fire him; only in that way could the clear responsibility of the President be maintained against congressional efforts to control the membership and procedures of the cabinet. I took his lecture on this principle to heart, even though I read a little later in Senator Watson's memoirs, *As I Knew Them*, that Vice-President Dawes, after their inauguration, sat regularly in Coolidge's cabinet. I never bothered to check on Senator Watson's accuracy.

As another former vice-president, Truman was more persuaded by Dawes's principles than his performance. When in order to get Republican support for the European Recovery Program (the Marshall Plan) he had to promise to put a Republican in charge, some early draft of the statute would have made that officer formally a member of the cabinet. The congressional legislative draftsmen objected on legal grounds: no statute had ever defined the cabinet membership or functions. The congressmen settled for a statutory phrase giving the officer in question "rank equivalent to that of the head of an Executive Department." Accordingly, when Paul Hoffmann was appointed to the job, Truman invited him to the next cabinet meeting. But when Hoffmann's secretary phoned the White House to find the date for the next one, she was told that he was not expected to attend. Nor, as it turned out, was he on the list for later meetings.

As noted in Chapter V, the debates over the coordination of diplomatic and military affairs of the period after World War II often focused attention on the possible creation by statute of a system of cabinet committees served by a cabinet secretariat. As a leader in the fight against unification of the military services and for the creation instead of the National Security Council with a statutory secretariat, Secretary Forrestal continued to argue for extension of that system to the whole range of federal policy. When he became a member of the first Hoover Commission he made this idea his primary purpose.

While I was skeptical about his views on this issue, I had great respect for his dedication to public service and for the breadth of his policy interests. Among those who came to Washington from private life for wartime service, he had an unusual commitment to strengthening the permanent institutions of government. My fear was that he, as a lawyer, was inclined to rely too heavily on a legalistic approach.

The story current at that time was that he undertook to show a famous admiral, back in Washington for his first visit after many months of combat service in the Pacific, the new Navy Department offices, greatly expanded to take care of the industrial mobilization and weapons procurement programs. In one big room he pointed to row on row of desks, all populated with Wall Street lawyers, pressed into civilian service for wartime duty. The admiral exclaimed incredulously, "My God, Mr. Secretary, are we fighting the Japs or suing them?"

Secretary Forrestal's interests were fortunately broader than Wall Street. He had, even during the war, become convinced that the federal government needed a civil service of higher quality and broader interests. Through a member of his staff, he had learned of my interest in the British civil service, and asked me to write for him a paper describing its major features and the extent to which it could profitably be imitated. When a few years later, he found that I was working under the Hoover Commission, of which he was a member, he asked for advice on another possible application of the British model to American institutions—in this case, the cabinet secretariat. After some discussion of the subject, in which I had made my skepticism clear, he surprised me by asking me to ghost-write an article for him on the subject. The process of writing and revising the article, to which he paid more attention in detail than I expected that the head of the largest federal department could afford, led him to reconsider his earlier views and accept the need for tying any secretariat of the sort to the President's constitutional position, rather than to the cabinet as a collective entity. When the article appeared in the *New York Times Magazine* of May 19, 1948, he insisted (contrary to my views on the ethics of ghost-writing) on acknowledging my collaboration.

While in the course of his study of the idea he had moderated and clarified his position considerably, it was not persuasive to those on the Hoover Commission who feared any move in the direction of formalizing the status of the cabinet. The most he could get was the tepid recommendation in the commission's report for a "staff secretary" in the White House to help the President manage the use of interdepartmental committees.

It was easy to sympathize (even while disagreeing) with the wish that in the U.S. we could get away from turbulent congressional politics and imitate the more decorous procedures of the parliamentary cabinet system. That wish kept coming up in one form or another; my friends in the Budget Bureau and I felt virtuous in opposing it as self-appointed defenders of the presidency. That role became hard to play when the wish was expressed by the President personally. President Eisenhower felt oppressed by the multiplicity of the roles he had to play, all the while under the pressure of congressional criticism. He noticed the problem especially when attending meetings abroad with other heads of governments: they, as prime ministers, did not have the ceremonial obligations of chiefs of state (*e.g.*, the British Queen or French president), nor did they have to carry the burdens of administration, which were handled by the career civil servants. But the American President was chief of state and general manager as well as head of the government.

Eisenhower accordingly asked the President's Advisory Committee on Government Organization (PACGO) to evaluate his idea that the U.S. should create a new statutory position, the First Secretary of the Government, under the President but over all other executive officers, to deal with international affairs. With such a title, he could represent the U.S. at international meetings of prime ministers—*first secretary* being a literal translation of that title—and the President would be spared that obligation, and much of the burden of coordinating the executive departments.

After my work on Defense Department organization, I had been asked to serve as a consultant to PACGO, and this idea of a First Secretary seemed to me the most important issue before the committee, of which Nelson A. Rockefeller was chairman and Arthur Flemming and Milton Eisenhower (the President's brother) were the only other members. They let me in on the act, even knowing my skepticism. I feared that if Congress were to set up such a position, it could then oversee its occupant's work, and the presidency would be dangerously divided.

I argued that, if anything of the sort were to be considered, the President should think about delegating a greater role to the member of his cabinet with, historically, the widest and most flexible range of duties—the secretary of state, whose role had originally encompassed many domestic functions and who still handled for the President governmentwide ceremonial duties such as issuing presidential appointments and enrolling acts of Congress. By tradition, Congress specified the duties of the secretary of state in much less detail than those of any other secretary. If a new job could be created for a secretary of foreign affairs to run the State Department, the President could bring the secretary of state into the White House to be his righthand deputy, with authority granted only by delegation, not by statute.

It was too slick an idea. I was taken to the Oval Office with the committee in June, 1957, as it proposed the scheme as a better way to do what the President wanted. He was annoyed, scolded the lot of us, and sent us back to do what he wanted. It never got done. When Rockefeller resigned his federal responsibilities to run for the governor's office in New York, I was designated as a member (though not the chairman) of PACGO. We always had more practical problems on our hands, and although the committee had presented the President with draft plans to carry out his scheme, political difficulties always seemed to prevent action. Several years later Governor Rockefeller repeatedly revived the First Secretary idea and presented it as his own recommendation, first in public speeches in 1960 and then in 1964 by letters recommending it to President Johnson and to the Senate Judiciary Committee. But nothing ever came of the proposal.

1. Report of the President's Committee on Administrative Management, 1937; see also Louis Brownlow, "A General View," *Public Administration Review*, I (Winter, 1941), 102.

2. Commission on Organization of the Executive Branch of the Government, *General Management of the Executive Branch: A Report to the Congress* (Washington, D.C., February, 1949).

3. Subcommittee on Employee Ethics and Utilization of the Committee on Post Office and Civil Service, House of Representatives, *Presidential Staffing—a Brief Overview*, 95th Cong., 2nd Sess., Committee Print No. 95–17, July 25, 1978. An exception to the failure of Presidents to act to reduce the size of the Executive Office was the action by President Nixon in Reorganization Plan No. 1 of 1973. See *Hearing Before a Subcommittee of the Committee on Government Operations*, 93rd Cong., 1st Sess., February 26, 1973, p. 7.

4. President's Advisory Council on Executive Organization (Ash Council), Memorandum for the President, "The Executive Office of the President—an Over-

view," October 26, 1970. This memorandum warned the President that his Executive Office was becoming a miscellany of irrelevant activities instead of an agency of staff support, simply because special interests wanted the prestige of location there.

5. Donald Haider, "The Presidential Management Initiatives: A Ford Legacy to Executive Management Improvement," *Public Administration Review*, XXXIX (No. 3, 1979), 259 n.

6. Louis Fisher, "Congress and the President in the Administrative Process: The Uneasy Alliance," in Hugh Heclo and Lester M. Salamon (eds.), *The Illusion of Presidential Government*, (Boulder, Colo., 1981), 21–44.

7. For a carefully qualified comment on savings, see President's Committee on Administrative Management, *Administrative Management in the Government of the United States* (Washington, D.C., 1937), 51. The contrasting emphasis of the Hoover Commission was made clear by the campaign of the volunteer organizations set up to advocate adoption of its reports. Their approach was typified by the endorsement of the McGraw-Hill Book Company, which published a compilation of the major reports of the commission and estimated in a preface signed by "The Publishers" that their adoption would make cash savings of more than $3 billion a year. *The Hoover Commission Report* (New York, n.d.).

8. William D. Carey, "Presidential Staffing in the Sixties and Seventies," *Public Administration Review* (September–October, 1969), 450–58. For an appraisal of the budget staff under Harold Smith, see Allen Schick, "The Problems of Presidential Budgeting," in Heclo and Salamon (eds.), *Illusion of Presidential Government*, 87–91.

9. "The President's Message to the Congress Transmitting Reorganization Plan 2 of 1970, Implementing Recommendations of the President's Advisory Council on Executive Organization, March 12, 1970," *Weekly Compilation of Presidential Documents*, March 16, 1970, pp. 353–57.

10. For President's Committee on Administrative Management, see Charles E. Merriam, "The National Resources Planning Board," *Public Administration Review*, I (Winter, 1941), 116–20, and Harold D. Smith, "The Bureau of the Budget," *ibid.*, 112.

11. Commission on Organization of the Executive Branch of the Government, *Task Force Report on Personnel and Civil Service* (Washington, D.C., 1955), 7, 8; Commission on Organization of the Executive Branch of the Government, *Personnel and Civil Service: A Report to the Congress* (Washington, D.C., 1955).

12. Fritz Morstein Marx, "The Bureau of the Budget: Its Evolution and Present Role," *American Political Science Review*, XXXIX (No. 4), 653, (No. 5), 869.

13. *Public Administration Times*, IV (May 1, 1981). The director of the Office of Personnel Management, Donald Devine, a year later reaffirmed and clarified his point at a panel discussion in Washington, as reported in *Bureaucrat* (Spring, 1982), 19–22.

14. Philip Shabecoff, "U.S. Closes Unit That Cited Health Effect of Lead in Gas," *New York Times*, July 26, 1982, p. A8.

15. For an appraisal of Merriam's and Brownlow's contributions to policy planning, see Barry D. Karl, *Charles E. Merriam and the Study of Politics* (Chicago, 1974), and Karl, *Executive Reorganization and Reform in the New Deal* (Cambridge, Mass., 1963). See also, Sir Henry Noel Bunbury, *Governmental Planning Machinery* (Chicago, 1938).

16. Corinne Silverman, "The President's Economic Advisers," in *Case Studies in American Government* (Englewood Cliffs, N.J., 1962).

17. Edward J. Burger, *Science in the White House: A Political Liability?* (Baltimore, 1980).

18. Committee on Armed Services, U.S. Senate, *Report of the Rockefeller Committee on Department of Defense Reorganization*, Committee Print, 83rd Cong., 1st Sess., April 11, 1953.

19. Bruce L. R. Smith, *The Rand Corporation: Case Study of a Nonprofit Advisory Corporation* (Cambridge, Mass., 1966).

20. For a summary report on the abortive effort to establish an "Institute for Congress," see *Science*, October 4, 1974, p. 37. The case for the Institute's creation was stated by Alton Frye before the Joint Committee on Congressional Operations, June 18, 1974.

21. *National Journal*, January 24, 1981, p. 128, describes "Right-of-Center Defense Groups—The Pendulum Has Swung Their Way."

22. New York *Times*, March 17, 1982, p. A20.

23. Personal interviews with Secretary Marshall and with General Lord Ismay, military secretary to the British Cabinet, 1948. General Marshall's views on this issue are confirmed by Forrest C. Pogue, *George C. Marshall, Organizer of Victory* (New York, 1973), 5, 69–70, and 197–98.

24. "A System of Coordination in the Executive Branch of the United States," J.C.S. 1555, October 18, 1945 (MS in Modern Military Branch, Military Archives Division, National Archives and Records Service). For background on the British War Cabinet system and its impact on American thought and practice, see Franklyn A. Johnson, *Defence by Committee* (London, 1960), esp. 295–303, 315–38.

25. Maurice Hankey, *Government Control in War* (Cambridge, 1945). Secretary Forrestal's concern with the problem was elaborated later in his article "If the Government Is Really to Do a Job—" *New York Times Magazine*, May 9, 1948.

26. William F. Willoughby, *Government Organization in War Time and After* (New York, 1919), Chap. 1.

27. Albert A. Blum, "Birth and Death of the M-Day Plan," in Harold Stein (ed.), *American Civil-Military Decisions: A Book of Case Studies* (Birmingham, Ala., 1963).

28. Merle Miller, *Plain Speaking—an Oral Biography of Harry S. Truman* (New York, 1973), 199.

29. Pogue, *George C. Marshall*, 70.

30. President Truman told this story in his *Years of Trial and Hope* (New York, 1956), Chap. 4.

31. William Y. Elliott, *The Need for Constitutional Reform: A Program for National Security* (New York, 1935).

32. This paper, which is described in Hugh Heclo, "Organization Trends in the Executive Office of the President" (Research Report No. 3 prepared for the National Academy of Public Administration Presidential Management Project 5), may be found in Official File, Appendixes OF 101 and 101b, "Power of the President, 1941–45," Roosevelt Presidential Library.

33. Karl, *Merriam and the Study of Politics*, 253, 254. The Brownlow paper was similar in many respects to the proposal by Professor Elliott several years earlier. It differed, however, in putting more emphasis on staffing the secretariat by career officers rather than political appointees and in avoiding, or trying to avoid, any interference by Congress in its internal operations. The break between the Brownlow Committee and Elliott was less the result of substantive disagreement than of a clash of personalities. Unlike the other staff members of the Brownlow Committee, Professor Elliott chose to go directly to President Roosevelt with his ideas; the President, however, found the Brownlow approach more compatible with his own.

34. Commission on Organization of the Executive Branch of the Government, *General Management of the Executive Branch*, 17–23. This general principle was supported by the Ash Council. See President's Advisory Council on Executive Organization; Memorandum for the President, "Proposed Organization of the Executive Office of the President," October 17, 1969.

35. Nelson Rockefeller, after leaving the chairmanship of the President's Advisory Committee on Government Organization to become governor of New York, told in a public speech about having taken part in studies for the President of the problems of coordination in international affairs and went on to describe the proposed position of First Secretary of the Government, which would by statute be given the responsibility as executive chairman of the National Security Council and empowered to represent the President on the prime ministerial level at international conferences. (Address in Binghamton, N.Y., on June 21, 1960, text released by press secretary to the governor, Albany.) The address was reported and discussed by Hanson W. Baldwin in the New York *Times*, June 24, 1960. The records of the recurrent discussions of this idea may be found in the files of minutes and notes of meetings of the President's Advisory Committee on Government Organization, in the Dwight D. Eisenhower Presidential Library, Abilene, Kans.: see Box 3, Unit 20, 1956; Box 11, unit 72 (Management and International Affairs; First Secretary and Office of Executive Management, 1959–60); and Box 12, unit 93 (Foreign Affairs, etc., 1954–57).

36. *Weekly Compilation of Presidential Documents*, March 16, 1970, p. 354.

37. For a description of the Economic Policy Board under President Ford, see Roger B. Porter, *Presidential Decision-Making* (Cambridge, 1980). Porter, who served on the staff of that board, later became office director of the Office of Policy Development in the White House in the Reagan administration. The general theory of cabinet committees that the Economic Policy Board exemplified seems to have been followed by the Reagan committees.

38. President's Committee on Administrative Management; see Brownlow, "A General View," 102; Lewis Meriam and Laurence F. Schmeckebier, *Reorganization of the National Government—What Does It Involve?* (Washington, D.C., 1939); W. F. Willoughby, *An Introduction to the Study of the Government of Modern States* (New York, 1909), 229–31, 252, 351. Willoughby's conclusion was that the Constitution made the President chief executive, but not "administrator-in-chief." The latter position he got "merely because the legislative branch, in which final authority in respect to the organization and work of the administrative branch is vested, has as a matter of policy, made of this officer one to serve in this capacity" (351).

39. President's Committee on Administrative Management, *Administrative Management in the Government*, 44.

Chapter VI. Accountability Under the Unwritten Constitution

After the Eisenhower administration, Presidents continued to affirm their faith in what they loosely called cabinet government, but their reliance on their immediate staffs rather more than on their department heads continued to grow. I now suspect that this came about because of the pressure for instant answers from the growing congressional staffs and from television reporters and their tendency to personify decisions in terms of presidential politics. The change became apparent to me as a consultant and part-time staff member. President Kennedy may have wanted at least some appearance of continuity with his predecessor; so when he abolished the President's Advisory Committee on Government Organization, he substituted for it a panel of four advisers on the subject, of whom I was the only carry-over. But the panel never met, and its members as individuals were used most sparingly. The President's counsel and special assistants were too sophisticated to need us to instruct them that the issues of organization at the top level were matters of policy objectives and not of routine managerial economy.

The one field in which the old advisory system carried over, at least in appearance, was in scientific advice. Scientists, unlike public administrators, were a constituency too powerful to be ignored. Because of my acquaintance with that field, I found myself in a channel of communication between Senator Henry Jackson's staff, which was eager to see some changes made in the attitude of scientists to national security, and the old leadership of the President's Science Advisory Committee. The outcome, over which my influence was zero, was to have a new chairman—Jerome Wiesner instead of George Kistiakowsky—but otherwise to keep the PSAC membership.

I had gone to Harvard in 1958 and watched with some envy some of my new colleagues there take off for the Washington scene where I would still have felt more at home. The one whose position was later to typify the growing power of White House staff was the President's national security adviser, McGeorge Bundy, who left the top deanship (arts and sciences) at Harvard and took with him my colleague in our Science and Public Policy Program, Carl Kaysen. Their relationship to the President and the secretary of state was a hint of what was to come later; in principle, I suspect, they would have affirmed that the secretary should be the President's principal agent in foreign affairs, but when the President wanted instant action under his own intimate direction they were not about to hold back. So their role became quite different from that of James Lay, who ran the National Security Council staff under Truman, or Robert Cutler under Eisenhower but was still restrained by comparison with that of Kissinger or Brzezinski in later years.

After the death of President Kennedy, President Johnson set up in the summer of 1964—an election year—a number of so-called task forces to advise him after the election on various aspects of policy or program. I was asked to chair the one on government reorganization. We were different from the others not only in our subject matter but because we maintained an old-fashioned attitude to the advisory function: we refused to leak our recommendations to the press. We were not old-fashioned, however, in our analysis of the problem or in our recommendations. We affirmed that reorganization should not be assigned for study to a new "Hoover Commission" since its main purpose was not managerial economy but rather the adjustment of structure to the development of new purposes and policies, which in turn required more sophisticated program analysis and review and more attention to new scientific and technological developments.

This emphasis, we urged, made it important to distinguish carefully between the role of the executive departments, which had to be accountable to the Congress as well as to the President, and that of the Executive Office, which should be divested of the operating authority and responsibilities that had been assigned to it and made a smaller and more strictly a staff agency to the President. We also recommended reform of the higher civil service in terms that anticipated the Civil Service Reform Act of 1978.

We were better in outlining what should be done than in cultivating a connection with the officer who had to do it, the President. After the election, President Johnson invited to dinner those who had chaired the several task forces. In my innocence, I expected that this would be the chance to discuss with him the substance of our recommendations. But when we sat down to dinner Vice-President Humphrey was acting as our host, and the President turned up only in the middle of the evening. By that late hour, there would hardly have been time for a score of us advisers to talk in any detail about our interests, but that was not the problem: the President did not want to listen at all to us, but to lecture us—especially those of us from academic institutions—about the shameful way intellectuals were tolerating the attacks of radical students on his conduct of the Viet Nam War. Even though at Harvard I had been within the wing of the faculty that was considered ultraconservative on the issues posed by the student riots, I felt obliged to interpose timidly and suggest that there was something to be said for the students' concerns about Viet Nam. If I had ever had any future role as a White House adviser, that ended my chances.

I am sure that the President never read the report of our task force. His staff did so and several of the subsequent actions of the administration were in line with (whether or not they were influenced by) our recommendations—for example, the creation of the Department of Transportation and the abolition of the Atomic Energy Commission. But they had been on the agenda of the Budget Bureau for years, and no one can ever say with confidence whether our ideas about program development and accountability were persuasive or whether we had simply been summarizing a consensus that had been developing among students of the subject.

More and more observers were coming to believe that the President's function as a manager for purposes of economy was less important than his policy leadership and that it was as necessary to provide for the accountability of the executive as for its efficiency. These ideas were in the atmosphere when the National Academy of Public Administration organized its study of presidential management in 1980. Unlike the more important earlier studies, this one was conducted under private rather than official auspices, but most of its participants were men and women of practical governmental experience, rather than from mainly scholarly backgrounds. Rocco Siciliano, who had been personnel adviser to President Eisenhower and under secretary of commerce under President Ford, was made one of the cochairmen of the panel, and I served as the other. The membership was bipartisan, including department heads and White House staff members from former Republican and Democratic administrations. Our report was completed just before the 1980 elections, and presented to both presidential candidates. After the election, we were confident that it had been read and considered carefully by the winning camp, but what its influence—if any—was, is a question I am content to leave to history.

1. Edmund Burke, "Reflections on the Revolution in France, and on the Proceedings of Certain Societies in London Relative to That Event," in *The Works of the Right Honourable Edmund Burke* (London, 1934), IV, 138.
2. National Academy of Public Administration, *A Presidency for the 1980s* (Washington, D.C., November, 1980).
3. Thomas Jefferson to Edward Carrington, August 4, 1787, in Adrienne Koch and William Peden (eds.), *The Life and Selected Writings of Thomas Jefferson* (New York, 1944), 428.
4. Lord Hailsham, a strong defender of the efficiency and integrity of the higher civil service in Great Britain, argues that the country's real problem is overcentralization: "the United Kingdom is far too large to be operated as a unitary state devoid of constitutional safeguards." Scottish nationalism, he believes, is sure to lead to further demands for federalism. *The Dilemma of Democracy* (London, 1978), 165.
5. Edith Stokey and Richard Zeckhauser, *A Primer for Policy Analyses* (New York, 1978), Chap. 13, show that although "a social welfare function exists in principle . . . we cannot provide a universally acceptable basis for its construction that is both logical and practical." Indeed, they say that "Kenneth Arrow has virtually demonstrated that we should give up the search. In *Social Choice and Individual Values* [New York, 1963], he proves that no wholly satisfactory procedure for combining individual preferences to produce a ranking for society as a whole can ever be found." They go on to say that the political problem is even more difficult than Arrow says, for he assumes that you discover peoples' preferences by asking them, but you can never be sure of getting candid answers, since one may frequently gain by misstating his preferences.
6. William D. Carey, "Dilemmas of Scale," *Science*, June 18, 1982, p. 1277.
7. Lawrence Kohlberg, "From Is to Ought," in T. Mischel (ed.), *Cognitive Development and Epistemology* (New York, 1971).
8. Ronald Dworkin, *Taking Rights Seriously* (Cambridge, Mass., 1978); Charles Fried, *Right and Wrong* (Cambridge, Mass., 1978).
9. Burke, "Reflections on the Revolution in France," 67–68.
10. Walter Bagehot, *The English Constitution* (1867; rpr. London, 1933), Chap. 1.
11. John Milton, "On the New Forcers of Conscience Under the Long Parliament," in Andrew J. George (ed.), *The Shorter Poems of John Milton* (New York, 1898).

Index

Index